Acclaim for

A THOUSAND FRIGHTENING FANTASIES...

"I will personally cherish this work, because I believe I will be able to use it to help others manage the ugly ogre of scrupulosity in their lives. If and when they do, they will discover something of that peace 'which surpasses all understanding.'"

— JOHN CARDINAL O'CONNOR
Archbishop of New York

"With the acuity, balance, and scholarship worthy of the late and, until now, the unequalled A. Gemelli, William Van Ornum brings to us the great moral drama of scrupulosity that has bedeviled humankind for centuries.

"Much has been said and written on scrupulosity and on obsessive compulsive disorder. No one has organized the subject so thoroughly, so gracefully, so eloquently, so tolerantly, and with such helpful scholarship as William Van Ornum. The collection of data from around the world from one thousand scrupulous people is a pioneering achievement.

"If you are scrupulous, if you know any scrupulous person, if you want to learn how to help a scrupulous person, read this volume."

— FRANK J. KOBLER, Professor Emeritus of Psychology
Loyola University of Chicago

"To those who wonder why he wrote this book, William Van Ornum might echo Pope John XXIII when he was asked why he convened Vatican Council II: 'To make the human sojourn on earth less sad.' This book will surely do that for countless men and women who have suffered not only the special pains of depression and religious scrupulosity but at times from the treatments prescribed for them. This is a very great practical handbook for this specific syndrome but, because of its tone of profound human understanding, it is something more, a book whose gentle and seasoned wisdom will make anybody who reads it feel better and more courageous about facing the challenges of life."

—EUGENE KENNEDY
Co-author of *On Becoming a Counselor*

"Scrupulosity is misunderstood, easily dismissed, and often seen as 'something that they (the scrupulous) can get over with just a little will power.' William Van Ornum clears away the misunderstanding, focuses our attention, and helps us understand what scrupulosity is, and what it is not. This book needs to be read by all priests, spiritual directors, and mental health personnel before they walk the journey with the scrupulous person entrusted to their care."

—REV. THOMAS M. SANTA, C.S.S.R.
Scrupulous Anonymous Director

"A thoughtful and clinically sensitive look at an aspect of moral and spiritual and psychological frailty."

—ROBERT COLES, psychiatrist and author of
The Call of Service: A Witness to Idealism

"God love you, Mr. Van Ornum, for your sincere desire to help people who are troubled in this way. I will pray that your book brings light and peace to many."

—MOTHER TERESA, M.C.
Calcutta, India

A THOUSAND
FRIGHTENING
FANTASIES

A THOUSAND FRIGHTENING FANTASIES

*Understanding and Healing Scrupulosity
and Obsessive Compulsive Disorder*

William Van Ornum

Foreword by
John Cardinal O'Connor

A Crossroad Book
The Crossroad Publishing Company
New York

1997

The Crossroad Publishing Company
370 Lexington Avenue, New York, NY 10017

Copyright © 1997 by William Van Ornum

Printed in the United States of America

Library of Congress Cataloging-in-Publication Data

Van Ornum, William.
    A thousand frightening fantasies : understanding and healing
scrupulosity and obsessive compulsive disorder / William Van Ornum :
foreword by John Cardinal O'Connor.
      p. cm.
    Includes bibliographical references and index.
    ISBN 0-8245-1605-2 (pbk.)
    1. Obsessive-compulsive disorder – Religious aspects. 2. Obsessive-
compulsive disorder – Treatment. 3. Scruples. 4. Religious
addiction. I. Title.
RC533.V36 1997
616.85'227–dc21   96-29581
                                             CIP

For
William and Thomas Van Ornum,
the best sons in the world!
May they remember always
that they are cherished
more than the lilies of the field

CONTENTS

FOREWORD

Psychiatrist Robert Coles of Harvard University expresses understandable perplexity that so many officials of so many churches refer their clergy for therapy instead of turning to the spiritual or sacramental resources within religion itself. I can testify to the phenomenon but am not surprised by it.

This brief reflection on Dr. William Van Ornum's *A Thousand Frightening Fantasies* is not the forum for exploring the reasons behind this phenomenon, but that many churches have suffered a loss of confidence in themselves seems undeniable. I myself meet periodically with a group of highly placed Catholic psychiatrists anxious for the insights of theology and faith, and sincerely reluctant to pretend to knowledge beyond their still limited field.

As one with a certain background in clinical psychology and psychiatry combined with more than fifty years of active priesthood, I am most grateful for what these sciences *do* offer, quite aware that neither faith nor theology is an adequate substitute when psychology or psychiatry is essential. The reverse of that truism, of course, is equally important.

In my judgment, one of the important contributions Dr. Van Ornum makes lies in his effort to promote a mutually rewarding marriage between the psychological and the religious. This particular contribution is basic to his analysis and proposed remedies for scrupulosity — that pebble in the shoe that makes walking fifty yards seem like fifty miles and, far worse, that cancer that eats away at every legitimate potential for joy in the human heart.

This book is well named, particularly if "a thousand" is translated as an infinite number, for, as the text observes, for every blip that goes off the radar screen of one's conscience, another instantly appears. The sufferer of scrupulosity is never, ever at peace for any length of time. Indeed, if peace steals into the heart unobserved, the scrupulous feel guilty over feeling peaceful, when they "know they don't deserve peace." I must confess to wondering, at times, whether the merry-go-round was invented by a sufferer of scrupulosity, compelled to do the same thing over and over and over, convinced of never getting it right.

If Dr. Van Ornum's book offers one hope — a hope I would underscore emphatically — it is that the scrupulous can be helped. Within the text the author is generous enough to quote a few informal suggestions I offered him while he was preparing the manuscript. I hope they bring hope to some sufferer somewhere.

I will personally cherish this work, not because it references me in passing, but because I believe I will be able to use it to help others manage the ugly ogre of scrupulosity in their lives. If and when they do, they will discover something of that peace "which surpasses all understanding."

JOHN CARDINAL O'CONNOR

PREFACE

This book is written for people with scrupulosity. They know they have it. They may not be aware of helpful therapies and medication. They may find it hard to sort out claims made by mental health professionals. For them I write this book and hope it represents one stop on their journey of healing. In writing this book, I have tried to serve as their advocate. Throughout the book I've tried to offer an honest evaluation of therapies for people with scrupulosity. Material of a more technical nature, of interest to therapists or academicians, is cited in the end notes.

Others will benefit from learning more about scrupulosity/obsessive compulsive disorder (Scrup/OCD). Family members need to know why someone they love acts so strangely at times. Perhaps therapists will be helped by learning more about scrupulosity as a distinct form of OCD. They may be surprised to learn of its existence during the past five hundred years. Medication and behavior therapies help many. There is a need for openness to other approaches as well, especially from a spiritual perspective, and I discuss this during the latter half of the book.

New developments in brain imaging tools are making it possible to locate changes in brain functioning due to medication or behavior therapy. I hope this book encourages researchers to consider expert talk therapy and spiritual approaches as variables in future research.

I am grateful to Scrupulous Anonymous. Over a thousand members responded to a four-page survey. Father Patrick Kaler provided help and encouragement. Father Thomas Santa continued Father Kaler's assistance.

My students and colleagues at Marist College deserve thanks and gratitude. Heidi Askin and Yves Paultre, newly minted school psychologists, devoted over a thousand hours each to statistical tasks and to American Psychological Association presentations in Boston, Washington, and Toronto. I appreciate their intelligence, hard work, and comradeship. Dr. Royce White provided extensive assistance on the statistical procedures and ongoing friendship and support. Dr. John Scileppi gave freely of his time to review the book in progress. My administrators at Marist College — Doctors William Eidle, Marc vanderHeyden, Mark Sullivan, and Dennis Murray — encourage my teaching and writing. They create an atmosphere of freedom of research inquiry unmatched anywhere.

My parents, Wesley and Shirley Van Ornum, have provided a strong foundation for my professional work. My father's honesty and sense of integrity are matchless, and my mother's sensitivity to others is a quality I can only hope to emulate. I am grateful that these qualities have been passed along to me and I hope their presence remains in future generations.

I am grateful to these people for interviews or other help on this project: Edna Foa, Steven Levenkron, Deborah Widmar, Grace Austen, Father Joseph Campo, Father Russell Abata, Paul Pressman, Robin Torres, John Mordock, Edward O'Keefe, Kathleen Zraly, Susan Muto, Christopher Brown, Maya Machocek, and Dr. Jack Sherman.

Various professional experiences helped me write this book. Dr. Frank Kobler of Loyola University of Chicago encouraged me in 1975 to continue in William James's tradition. He has helped me throughout this book through long-distance correspondence which has enriched the book immeasurably. Courses in theology taken at DePaul University piqued my interest in religious issues. While I was at Loyola in clinical psychology, Dr. Eugene Kennedy and Dr. Gerard Egan taught me about the intersection of psychology and pastoral counseling.

The openness of Thomas Merton to ideas from many branches of knowledge has always inspired me, and I hope the diversity reflected in the references list contributes helpful ideas to understanding scrupulosity and obsessive compulsive disorder.

I am grateful to John Cardinal O'Connor, Bishop Howard J. Hubbard, Mother Teresa, Joseph Cardinal Bernardin, and Christopher Brown — all of whom guided and encouraged spiritual aspects of this book, an area where I am just a beginner.

The work of the OCD Foundation has been a beacon to many, and their efforts are recognized and commended.

Working thirteen years as a clinical psychologist has broadened my understanding of OCD and other problems. Over a decade of work at Astor Home for Children as a psychologist, administrator, and board member taught me the need to combine medical, behavioral, and talk therapies in general practice. Service as a New York State disability examiner and director of psychology at Craig House Hospital impressed on me the complexity of relationships of any psychiatric condition. As general editor of The Crossroad Counseling Series I learned to review critically the work of professionals and to strive to locate simple and helpful approaches. Teaching at Marist for twelve years encouraged me to interpret seemingly disparate information.

Special thanks to Michael Leach. Maxwell Perkins could not have been a better editor or mentor. I'm just one of hundreds of authors who say this. John Eagleson did a great job to make this book more organized and readable, and I thank him myself and on behalf of the reader.

Extra special thanks are due to Lori Rivenburgh, M.A. When carpal tunnel syndrome struck, Lori provided great help in typing and consolidating the manuscript. Thank you, Lori!

A THOUSAND
FRIGHTENING
FANTASIES

Part One

HOW IT WAS

The five chapters of Part One deal with scrupulosity as a form of obsessive compulsive disorder that has been described during the past five hundred years. Current psychological and spiritual writers stress the importance of viewing human experience from both the male and female perspective. During past history and in current times, scrupulosity has been expressed differently by the two sexes.

A theme in the lives of many great historical figures has been the presence of an understanding and directive counselor or spiritual guide. This lesson from history is reaffirmed in the stories of contemporary sufferers of scrupulosity in chapters 6 through 9. While current psychiatric practice has brought tremendous relief to many sufferers of scrupulosity and obsessive compulsive disorder, current researchers may overlook the importance of a long-term trusting and caring relationship in the lives of people with scrupulosity and obsessive compulsive disorder. History teaches us a wider perspective.

Chapter 3 presents previously unavailable scientific research on scrupulosity that was completed just before World War I. This data, combined with the results of the studies leading to this book, suggests that scrupulosity and obsessive compulsive disorder are genetic disorders with multifactorial inheritance (described below on p. 137) — one that can be influenced both by genes and environment. This provides great hope for effective medical and psychological treatments.

Chapter 1

A STORY OF SCRUPULOSITY

The task of understanding scrupulosity provides drama and a good story. What is scrupulosity? Those who suffer from it know it instantly. Others such as family members, friends, work colleagues, and most mental health professionals have never heard of it. Some define scrupulosity as excessive worry and concern over religious matters.

John Cardinal O'Connor suggests a wider definition: "You can call scrupulosity an obsessive compulsive behavior, but clearly people become scrupulous over a broad spectrum of issues which are not explicitly religious. Because of the moral sensitivity of their conscience, people scruple over the moral dimensions of daily behavior" (Interview with John Cardinal O'Connor, January 23, 1996).

Scrupulosity afflicts mostly Roman Catholics but also affects others such as Orthodox Jews, Protestants, and Muslims.[1] This book looks especially at Catholic scrupulosity, but the underlying themes and dynamics apply to all religions.[2] Scrupulosity has probably existed since the beginning of time, and religious writers have clearly defined it during the past five hundred years. The research leading to this book discovered that scrupulosity in Catholics is a unique manifestation of obsessive compulsive disorder. Over ten thousand people participated in this research, and more than one thousand completed intensive survey information.[3] Examples of scrupulosity include:

- Martha, age forty-six, is a computer programmer. Martha stays at work after everyone has gone home. She feels she does not give her employer 100 percent effort during the day and staying late is an act of restitution. This annoys her husband.

- Robert, age twenty-three, goes to confession every week. He has "bad thoughts," mostly in church, involving what he thinks is blasphemous. These trouble him greatly.

- Alicia, age seventy, stated, "I have been scrupulous for fifty years. It robbed my life of fun and joy." Alicia worries about germs, particularly *after* she uses the toilet, because she fears she may contaminate others — a sin.

- Jake, age fifty-six, says his rosary exactly three times each morning. Doing this, he believes, keeps him from acting crazy at work.

There is an unrecognized presence of scrupulosity among the general population, as researchers Heidi Askin, Yves Paultre, and Royce White have discovered. Cardinal O'Connor agrees: "Priests who were trained prior to the Second Vatican Council at least had some sense of scrupulosity. They were taught about it in moral theology. They recognized it pretty quickly in the confessional" (Interview with John Cardinal O'Connor, January 23, 1996).

Some suggest that scrupulosity is less prevalent since Vatican II. Cardinal O'Connor offers a differing insight: "I think tremendous numbers of things are blamed on the Second Vatican Council. But this in my judgment is a complete misconstruction of the Council. A huge number of people talk about the spirit of the Second Vatican Council but you could walk down any street in New York, the most crowded street in New York, all day long and find only the tiniest handful of people who have read the documents from the Second Vatican Council.

In many cases, the sacrament of Penance, Reconciliation, and confession weren't even treated. The whole idea of sin, as Dr. Menninger said, just kind of disappeared from our vocabulary and our conceptualization. Whatever happened to sin?

And I think that a number of seminaries were caught up in this and a certain number of seminarians, and therefore priests, were raised in this mentality. That was not the intention of the Second Vatican Council in my judgment at all.

Since Vatican II, the discussion on scrupulosity has waned, but scrupulosity still exists. I think readers might want to reflect briefly on what I suspect might be a reason.

A certain number of priests, a certain number of post–Vatican II priests, spent far less time in the confessional. I'm not saying this as an indictment. This is simply the way things were. They spent far less time in the confessional and a good bit of time in taking courses and sometimes pseudo-courses in counseling. Then some, certainly not all of these priests, in turn became, and this may sound harsh, pseudo-counselors instead of spiritual directors or confessors. Some of them, I regret to say, simply didn't know what they were doing. Some were merely mouthing a good bit of Carl Rogers material. They had no true philosophic or psychological understanding of the dynamics of the human personality. A lot of jargon and pop psychology about feeling right and how not to feel guilty and so on filled the air of the day.

You don't help a truly scrupulous individual by saying "Well, you shouldn't feel bad." That doesn't do it, and you can compound the scrupulosity with such an approach.

(Interview with John Cardinal O'Connor,
January 23, 1996)

This book suggests consideration of these approaches when treating scrupulosity: (1) behavior therapy; (2) medication; (3) directive and expert talk therapy; (4) knowledge of healthy and realistic religious practices; (5) encouragement of positive and healthy spirituality.

This book, written by a clinical psychologist, uses different methods to study scrupulosity. People suffering from scrupulosity participated in two studies. The first study examined scrupulosity and obsessive compulsive disorder and a host of other personality qualities. A second study, in 1995, focused on new medications available since 1989. These surveys, using scientific principles, offer a detailed exploration into this puzzling and bedeviling condition.

The information yielded from these surveys comprises only part of this story. The survey provided rich data concerning scrupulosity, but material from extremely diverse sources — old books discovered in monastery libraries, four-color pamphlets from pharmaceutical companies, scientific studies by Ivy League scientists, newsletters from self-help groups, a new catechism from the pope — created the final story.

A second approach harnesses the openness of William James. Unlike many if not most psychologists in the past century, James was intrigued by the study of religion, and he longed for peace with God. His empathic and compassionate outlook embraced the religious experiences of people all over the world. He wrote the classic *The Varieties of Religious Experience*. While James's empathy is one helpful component of his phenomenology, other aspects of his thought in life suggest he never reached a state of psychological and spiritual peace. His doubting and inability to take a leap of faith — characteristics of scrupulosity and obsessive compulsive disorder — left him spiritually adrift and unfulfilled.

St. Ignatius, like modern-day behavioral psychologists, recognized that the treatment of scrupulosity required direction. Cardinal O'Connor noted:

> St. Ignatius had a fundamental principle that you may be familiar with — *Age quod agis*, "Do what you're doing." He would say to give full intensity and your total presence to this moment. In the Spanish Civil War novel of many years ago, *The Cypresses Believe in God*, Ignace, as I recall, is the hero throughout. I think this hero was clearly named after Ignatius. There is a passage where Ignace's confessor gives him important advice. It was basically this *Age quod agis*.

A third approach employs a comprehensive historical review. It is surprising that theologians going back centuries depict scrupulosity with accuracy, but psychologists ignore this topic.[4] One autumn day I sent two of my graduate assistants to the library at Mount St. Alphonsus. This monastery center is named for St. Alphonsus Liguori, himself a sufferer of scrupulosity. The material on scrupulosity that they found there amazed them. It would never have turned up on even the most sophisticated psychology computer search.

Fourth, since the psychological profession esteems a "case study" approach as a time-honored method of inquiry, this book looks at individual people who suffer from scrupulosity and examines their lives closely. Sufferers of scrupulosity from all over the world shared stories of their lives.

These methods contribute to an objective as well as a subjective understanding of scrupulosity. But knowledge in itself is sterile, and must help others through application. Consequently, a fifth aspect of this book critically examines approaches to treating scrupulosity and OCD. At present, there is more help and hope available for sufferers of scrupulosity than at any time in past centuries. Since scrupulosity combines with obsessive compulsive behavior, many approaches of psychologists in treating obsessive compulsive disorder are helpful. However, mental health professionals who treat OCD differ sharply concerning its proper treatment. I will propose a new synthesis combining different methods, including medication treatments that have dramatically eased the anguish of some as well as healthy spiritual and religious practices (see chapter 15).

This book includes original interviews with therapists Edna Foa, Steven Levenkron, Abby Levenkron, Lesley Shapiro, and Kathleen Zraly. Bishop Howard J. Hubbard and John Cardinal O'Connor speak from a religious perspective. Dr. Jack Sherman discusses the genetic implications of his research, and Susan Muto reflects on the presence of scrupulosity among great women spiritual writers.

Edna Foa is a world-renowned researcher on obsessive compulsive disorder who directs a highly acclaimed OCD Clinic at the University of Pennsylvania Medical College. Her work is noted in chapter 11. Foa has "worked with many people who have religious scruples." While behavior therapy relieves many OCD sufferers of symptoms, Foa noted that "religious scruples can be more difficult to deal with because the ideas are hard to discredit." She emphasized that a common feature of effective treatment for all forms of obsessive compulsive disorder is to help the sufferers "do what they are most afraid to do."

Bishop Hubbard reflected on the range of approaches and offers inspiration in chapter 14, "The Lilies of the Field."

There is great optimism in treating anxiety disorders such as scrupulosity and obsessive compulsive disorder. I hope to extend awareness of treatments and offer observations for new combinations of treatment.

This book targets people who suffer from scrupulosity but who may not have sought out psychological treatment for their problem. Sometimes persons with a religious orientation fear going into therapy. They suspect the counselor will try to "talk them out" or otherwise rob them of belief. While this can be true, many therapists respect religion. The presence of competent therapists throughout the country is reassuring. Therapy and medication combined represent an untapped resource for many people with scrupulosity.

Renewed emphasis on the role of thinking in human behavior provides hope. Cognitive psychology — changing emotions by changing thoughts — shows promise. This optimistic worldview differs from many past approaches. A reasonable though unacknowledged use of cognitive therapy includes prayer (see chapter 15) and religious liturgy. For sufferers of Scrup/OCD, this opens up further optimism for healing in combining psychological, medical, and religious approaches.

I also hope that psychologists who lack a religious orientation or who scorn religion will review the material on scrupulosity with an open mind.

Persons from various ethnic and national backgrounds rightfully hold therapists accountable for understanding their background. Racial groups, women's groups, persons with differing sexual inclinations — all decry judgmentalism. They assert the need of having respect and openness toward their values and traditions. Scrupulosity expresses a unique cultural experience, rooted in Catholic and other religious experiences of past centuries. I think mental health workers require the same understanding of this cultural tradition as any other.

A family therapist writing in the *APA Monitor,* a monthly publication for some one hundred thousand psychologists, offered this guideline:

> Show you understand. Send the message that you are sensitive to their values and cultural identity. Encourage them to use their natural support systems — their religious beliefs or their value in the family structure, for example — to cope with problems. Support systems that grow out of a particular culture become very important in helping us mobilize people's strengths and helping us to get people to cope. (Giordano 1995)

The OCD Wars

The past hundred years among mental health professionals treating obsessive compulsive disorder has been a century of disagreement. Freud's literary masterpieces on the Rat Man and Wolf Man held sway through the middle part of the twentieth century: obsessions and compulsions diverted anger and sexuality from their primary targets. Augustinus Gemelli depicted scrupulosity with clarity, but his work has remained undiscovered by psychologists.[5] In the 1960s and 1970s behavioral psychologists emphasized that obsessions and compulsions controlled severe anxiety. During the past ten years, new and promising medications have brought relief to many sufferers with OCD. Many assert biochemical or genetic causes of OCD. While current psychiatric orthodoxy emphasizes these last two approaches, often with an omniscient attitude, this book provides an overview of many approaches; persons suffering from obsessive compulsive disorder benefit from all possible resources. Although many benefit from medication and behavior therapy, the smaller percentage of those who don't numbers in the millions. This presence evokes doubt concerning whether or not these two approaches offer the total cure.[6]

Current psychiatric orthodoxy excoriates Freud, his followers, and anyone who suggests psychoanalysis or talk therapy helps scrupulosity. From my perspective, each of the following statements is true: (1) many psychoanalysts have botched cases of people with OCD; (2) effective talk therapy by experienced therapists has directly helped some people with OCD or has enhanced behavior therapy or medication. This second statement needs greater recognition among sufferers and professionals.

Many remember Freud as arrogant and dogmatic. Yet he stood in awe and humility before the complexity of OCD and scrupulosity. His famous patient "The Wolf Man" experienced scrupulosity as part of his OCD.[7]

Freud recognized the small number of people he treated with OCD, and he looked to future workers to work toward solving the riddle. He displayed enthusiasm for biological treatments, and I think if he were alive today he would be using anti-OCD medications to bolster his own approach.

Freud's own words encourage all in the mental health professions to work together, pool resources, and combine expertise to make us skilled helpers. In 1909, Freud wrote in his "Notes upon a Case of Obsessional Neurosis":

> In these circumstances there is no alternative but to report the facts in the imperfect and incomplete fashion in which they are known and in which it is legitimate to communicate them. The crumbs of knowledge offered in these pages, though they have been laboriously collected, may not in themselves prove very satisfying; but they may serve as a starting point for the work of other investigators, and common endeavor may bring the success which is perhaps beyond the reach of individual effort." (Freud 1963, 3)

"How Do I Know I Have It?": What Is Scrup/OCD?

Until about 1987, mental health experts estimated that between one and two people per thousand had obsessive compulsive disorder. As for scrupulosity, I found no estimates of prevalence. Since these estimates of the rarity of this condition, newer calculations place the incidence of OCD at between 2 and 3 percent of the population, and there has been a growing awareness of the condition among the public (American Psychiatric Association 1992 [DSM IV], 203). Psychoanalyst Leon Salzman believes that some people display OCD qualities but not the full-blown disorder. This book helps readers and therapists to determine the presence of scrupulosity, OCD, a combination of the two, or Scrup/OCD and another condition. We are just beginning to recognize the complex interactions in conditions such as OCD, attention deficit disorder, depression, and other problems of mood and thinking.[8]

The American Psychiatric Association publishes a resource, *The Diagnostic and Statistical Manual of Mental Disorders IV*. This book classifies psychiatric problems and suggests treatment. Psychiatrists have revised this tome five times in the past seventy years. They currently don't list scrupulosity as a disorder but may in the future.[9]

A well-known textbook on abnormal psychology lists expressions of OCD as follows:

- *Obsessions* are recurrent, persistent ideas, thoughts, images, or impulses coming to awareness. Examples include ideas of contamination, dread, guilt, urges to kill, attack, injure, confess, or steal.

- *Ruminations* are forced preoccupations with thoughts about a particular topic, brooding, doubting, and waffling. Examples include spending days worrying about an exam, changes in tax laws, an upcoming decision, or the weather next summer.

- *Cognitive rituals* include sequences of mental acts needing to be done precisely. Examples include saying prayers a certain way, counting calories in food before being able to eat the food, repeating certain "magical" sayings.

- *Compulsive motor rituals* are time-consuming and may involve cleaning, eating, toileting, grooming, sexual activity, work performance, or athletic performance. Examples include touching objects a certain length of time, repeating handwashing and showering, checking of gas and electricity, and hoarding of objects.

- *Compulsive avoidances* involve avoiding a real-life activity and substituting a ritual. Examples include the student who must clean his apartment seven times before studying or an athlete compelled to dress and redress five times before a game (Carson et al. 1995).

These waste time and imprison. An observer or family member might think, "That's really silly. Why don't they just stop? All you need is will power." Individuals enmeshed in OCD's power find it difficult to stop.

Many display OCD characteristics, yet experience quality lives. When rituals, avoidances, or thoughts begin to take more time — thereby limiting other satisfying activities — therapists diagnose OCD.[10]

It is amazing that mental health workers have overlooked such a well-defined psychological condition as scrupulosity.[11] This book is based on a survey sent to ten thousand people with scrupulosity. The research presented eight criteria for scrupulosity as defined by St. Ignatius Loyola:[12]

1. Scruples concern events, blowing the incident way out of proportion, as when Ignatius worried about stepping "upon a cross formed by two straws." Fretting that putting on lipstick breaks the one-hour Communion fast is a scruple. Another equates laughing at an obscene joke with blasphemy.

2. Scruples invade the mind, as if from nowhere, and create imaginary problems. Real worries — unemployment, divorce, war — are not scruples.

3. Scrupulosity converts minor happenings into grave sins. Expressing mild anger to a store clerk qualifies.

4. Scrupulous people waffle, doubt, and create their own anxiety. "I doubt and yet do not doubt," St. Ignatius said. Psychologists call this extreme ambivalence. One survey respondent, a medical technologist, worried constantly about reading results precisely. To allay her doubt, she asked others for a second opinion. Often people with scrupulosity visit their parish priest or confessor for that second opinion.

5. Scrupulous people enjoy doubting. It is familiar and has a reassuring rhythm. St. Ignatius said: "There is temptation to enter into the wrangle of doubts and counterdoubts."

6. Peace eludes scrupulous people. Worry is everywhere. Fretting knows no bounds and "the argument between guilt and innocence never ends." Father O'Flaherty states:

> A scruple is like a colosseum. The battle between innocence and guilt goes on in the arena inside the circular building and all around the outside are doors leading into the ring. Several struggles may be going on at once and the audience of emotions are rooting vociferously for their favorite gladiators. The doors leading into the conflict are so many syllogisms proving that the incidents are or are not sins. No gladiator ever wins.... The audience never tires of rooting. At one time the fighters on the side of fear are winning; but soon anxiety dominates.

One respondent likened scruples to planes landing at Kennedy Airport. After a landing, another always pops into the flight controller's screen. Scrupulosity is an airport that's always open.

7. Scrupulous people terrorize themselves about their eternal future. They "try to settle the doubt about eternal welfare." Reassurance brings no relief. One respondent noted: "I've had OCD,

and I've had my OCD take the form of scrupulosity. The scrupulosity is worse. Not only are you afraid of life, you get terrified about being damned forever. It's hard to explain, but it's worse than OCD." Edna Foa says the "eternal dimension" of scrupulosity makes it more difficult to treat at times than "straight OCD" (Interview with Dr. Edna Foa, December 13, 1995).

8. Amazingly, "a scruple enters a mind which is healthy, normal, and free of pathological disorders." Ignatius and many respondents affirm this. Chapter 4 describes otherwise healthy and successful individuals who suffer from scrupulosity. These people remain embarrassed about their condition — a reason for the ignorance among the public about scrupulosity. Scrupulous people suffer silently.

A Brief Test for Scrupulosity

If you were born before Vatican II, you know it if you have it and you know it when you see it. Seminaries provided special training on scrupulosity to future priests. Since Vatican II the faithful and the secular ignore scrupulosity, but scrupulosity still exists.

Research leading to this book included designing a brief test to look for scrupulosity and measure its presence. As with all psychological tests, the researchers needed a norm group. This test surveyed members of Scrupulous Anonymous, an organization sponsored by Redemptorist priests. Over one thousand members sent in surveys and a random sample of this group provided norms.[13] Here are the true/false questions followed by a scoring key:

1. ___ I often know exactly what thoughts or deeds are concerning me.

2. ___ I am never sure what is causing my distress.

3. ___ My thoughts often have rational explanations.

4. ___ My thoughts have no rhyme or reason.

5. ___ Many times, at least weekly, I feel I have committed a serious sin.

6. ___ I worry that any action I take may be sinful.

7. ___ Many times I am puzzled if I have sinned or not.

8. ___ I am often confused by all my doubts.

9. ___ I find some enjoyment in determining my guilt or innocence.

10. ___ I am often caught in a cyclical pattern between guilt or innocence.

11. ___ I find myself continually trying to decide if I'm guilty of doing something wrong.

12. ___ I am often compelled to settle my doubts no matter how long it takes.

13. ___ I feel obligated to determine if my actions are sinful.

14. ___ I believe myself to be a healthy person.

15. ___ I feel my concerns are those of a crazy person.

To score, allow one point for each question answered in the following manner: 1T, 2F, 3T, 4F, 5T, 6F, 7T, 8T, 9T, 10T, 11F, 12T, 13T, 14T, 15F. This information compares your score to others taking the test:

Score	Designation	percent of group reporting this
0–7	Low	20.4
8–10	Mild	48.9
11–12	Moderate	23.3
13–15	Severe	1.9

Results of the Survey

We studied the relationship between scrupulosity, obsessive compulsive disorder, and other factors among the members of Scrupulous Anonymous.

Over one thousand members returned surveys. Some wrote narratives — sometimes twenty-five pages long — describing their lifelong battles. Others provided phone numbers so I could call them. This project yielded helpful data. I have reviewed hundreds of studies on obsessive compulsive disorder. Most use small groups: those going to a particular clinic, behavior therapy patients, medication study subjects. This data, using a large-scale international group, provides new information on scrupulosity and OCD.

We discovered that persons scoring high on a test of obsessive compulsive disorder usually scored high on a test of scrupulosity. Scrupulosity is a form of obsessive compulsive disorder — *a unique type of obsessive compulsive disorder: Scrup/OCD.* As a corollary, scrupulous people frequently display other OCD behaviors. People with obsessive compulsive disorder may have scrupulosity. They may avoid helpful treatments for OCD. They or their therapists may ignore or misdiagnose scrupulosity.

Our second finding — one that gives hope — is that for many scrupulosity abates. Many therapies help, including relationships with inspired therapists, medications, behavior therapies, and even reading books. Survey respondents ranked spiritual direction as the most helpful practice. This suggests that therapists need greater awareness of healthy spiritual practices.

Our third finding — one to give pause — depicts immense suffering and anguish caused by scrupulosity. For example, when at its worst, 32 percent of respondents noted a severe or very severe effect on friendships; 35 percent noted severe or very severe effects on school; 43 percent noted severe or very severe effects on work.

Perhaps most sad is that 50 percent reported that scrupulosity had a severe or very severe effect on romance; 54 percent noted a severe or very severe effect on marriage. As with any affliction, isolation magnifies suffering; close relationships promote healing.

Many people with Scrup/OCD believe they have wasted years. They lost friends, love, time with children, work, recreation and hobbies, and sacramental participation. This is tragic. Therapists working with people who suffer from OCD note that successful treatment frees up time.

A fourth finding notes the waxing and waning of Scrup/OCD over the lifespan of the sufferer, results consistent with OCD in general. This does not mean that the course of Scrup/OCD is inevitable. Treatment can diminish its power.

The Wisdom of William James

William James, American psychologist, suffered himself from psychological problems. He grew up in a family where intellectual brilliance was commonplace. To be a genius merely meant you fit in. James felt criticized and belittled by his brilliant father. He stood in the shadow of his brother, literary genius Henry James. William learned to doubt, fret, worry, become depressed, and yearn for peace. He is a kindred sufferer to those plagued by Scrup/OCD.

For other reasons William James is crucial to a better understanding of Scrup/OCD. First, as a psychologist he empathized with religious experiences and unlike other psychologists did not reject them. He encouraged the open-minded study of religion. He was a *phenomenologist* — looking at experiences with empathy and a view from the inside. Second, he obtained knowledge through systematic use of case studies, an approach of this book.

Scrupulosity and History

Scrupulosity is ancient. The Hebrew Torah (especially the Christian book of Deuteronomy) contains long lists of specific rules, religious observances, and cleaning rituals.

Within Catholicism, St. Veronica Guliani, St. Catherine of Siena, and Julian of Norwich suffered from scrupulosity. St. Ignatius Loyola, Jesuit founder, gave us beautiful descriptions of scrupulosity. He suffered intensely during his early adult life, and even later. Another doctor of the church, St. Alphonsus Liguori, suffered tremendously from Scrup/OCD. He responded with love toward other sufferers.

Scrupulosity affects Protestants, past and present. Martin Luther experienced Scrup/OCD. His cure for Scrup/OCD will surprise readers. With the emergence and growth of fundamentalist religions, it is possible that scrupulosity's presence will increase into the new millennium.

In the twentieth century, scrupulosity flourished within American Catholicism before Vatican II. The council hoped to emphasize Christ's love rather than fears, but it did not eradicate scrupulosity. The recent promulgation of a new catechism by

Pope John Paul II may evoke a new interest in scrupulosity. Over-all the *Catechism of the Catholic Church* affirms positive aspects of the Catholic faith and I think it can be a very helpful document for therapists who work with Catholic scrupulosity. However, some expressions of doctrine may evoke anxiety in people prone to scrupulosity, as I discuss in chapter 13.

Jewish persons suffer from scrupulosity also — particularly Orthodox Jews. Dietary regulations can evoke scrupulosity, as I discuss in the next chapter.

Past writers from all these traditions offer sufferers and therapists of Scrup/OCD a treasure of compassion and perspective.

"No One Ever Asked Us": Life Stories of Persons Who Suffer from Scrup/OCD

No One Ever Asked Us, by Trudy Festinger, struck me as profound and simple. Festinger surveyed children's responses to foster care. Well-meaning adults from Charles Dickens onward had written about separation of children from parents and gave advice. Festinger pioneered by asking the children directly. This book provides a similar first-hand view of Scrup/OCD.

Review of life stories indicates four patterns of Scrup/OCD experience. The first group — described in chapter 6 — is made up of individuals who function well, and Scrup/OCD enhances their integrity. They hide their Scrup/OCD tendencies and friends, colleagues, family, or even spouses do not know about their struggles.

The second group — described in chapter 7 — includes those for whom scrupulosity is a struggle. They report being robbed of life satisfactions.

A third group — treated in chapter 8 — are those who suffer the combination of Scrup/OCD and depression.

The fourth group — examined in chapter 9 — contains persons bedeviled by Scrup/OCD. They are weary from other serious conditions. They tax themselves and their helpers. For their long-term healing and peace, they need complex treatment. Pastors, professional helpers, and family members must be alert to recognize if a sufferer of Scrup/OCD is in this group. Chapter 10 helps counselors diagnose the presence and extent of scrupulosity and other conditions and provides sufferers with an overview of what to expect from a mental health professional.

If you suffer from Scrup/OCD yourself, the articulate accounts in chapters 6–9 will let you know that you are not alone. These stories provide greater insights for therapists, physicians, pastoral workers, and family members.

What Can Be Done?

Effective therapies and competent physicians, therapists, and spiritual directors provide sound hope for persons with Scrup/ OCD. This book offers a synthesis of all approaches and practical guidelines, specific helps, and special encouragement from a compassionate Catholic bishop.

Cardinal O'Connor offers these thoughts for people who suffer from Scrup/OCD:

> I would very strongly affirm and reinforce that there is reason for optimism and reason to feel encouraged. As understanding of scrupulosity and obsessive compulsive disorder has improved immensely, so has the ability to get the kind of professional help that is so often needed.
>
> It is my personal conviction that it is really tragic to permit scrupulosity to go unattended and simply to try to live with it. It's a cancer.
>
> Horace used a Latin phrase, and the best you can translate it into English is "The dreadful dropsy increases by indulging itself." (*Crescit indulgens sibi dirus hydrops.*) The tremors of Parkinson's Disease, as one yields to them, seem to create and fortify a neuropattern that makes it get worse all the time. And that's what happens, I think, in scrupulosity.

This book is devoted to understanding, treating, healing, and battling scrupulosity and obsessive compulsive disorder.

Chapter 2

A VIEW FROM THE INSIDE

People with Scrup/OCD in the survey expressed loneliness and feeling apart from others. Many never met another person like themselves. Many longed to talk with a kindred spirit. It helps to know someone who has traveled your road in shoes like yours. This chapter shows what it is like to suffer from scrupulosity. I'm grateful to survey respondents who wrote so eloquently and hope this chapter broadens the understanding of family members and therapists.

• *They hide their scruples.* People with Scrup/OCD think they are weird. Even as children, they recognize that they are different. One respondent wrote:

> *I was eleven and everybody was playing baseball, having fun. I knew I was the only kid that was worrying about mortal sin. I wished I could just play and have fun like everyone else. Once I told the sister in school about this. She said with harshness in her voice, "You've got to stop worrying about this."*

This respondent discovered understanding fifteen years later when he entered therapy.

Several respondents reported a predicament when they became engaged. They wondered, "Should I tell my fiancé? How much should I say? Will he break it off when he learns?"

One respondent reported fears that his friends don't know:

> *I worry excessively about breaking the Communion fast. When I receive Communion, I worry about particles of the Host remaining on my hand. I worry about bad thoughts. I worry about breaking the church law about the Sabbath. These concerns take the joy out of my life.*

Some respondents over eighty years old said they hid their scrupulosity for their entire life. I hope that this book encourages anyone who has avoided seeking help to consider obtaining help to ease their anguish.

• *They worry selectively.* For many, scruples affect limited parts of life, but they are able to handle many other aspects of their lives in a nonscrupulous manner. Many who worry about the sinfulness of their thoughts lead functioning lives.

One respondent who reported success in her everyday life described this selective worry:

> *When I go to Mass, I must be perfect. There must be no rips in my clothes. I worry if the priest or deacon does his job right. Is it a valid Mass? The dismissal prayers cause me concern. I worry that the deacon forgot to say "The Mass is ended" or said the words in the wrong order.*

Another respondent stated:

> *My major problem is if I have been near or think I have been near raw red meat or blood. I can't grocery shop normally. I can't cook meat myself, but can enjoy a meal if someone else has cooked it.*

This person handles other life tasks in a normal manner.

• *Internally, they curse God.* Many with Scrup/OCD radiate anger and bitterness toward God. Internally, they curse their condition. They wonder why God selected them for torment. Since they are scrupulous, this bitterness evokes greater anguish. Guilt follows.

Scrupulosity is a snare that traps many. Many respondents felt they committed the sin against the Holy Spirit. This offense, mentioned briefly in the New Testament, suggests a type of alienation from God that even God won't forgive. This misery is endless.

One man stated:

> *My image of God is a punishing God. I feel He watches my every move and waits for me to sin. He marks it in a book in Heaven. I cannot escape the punishment I know I deserve.*

The experience of this man represents the unrelenting anguish of scrupulosity in its severe form.

Elisabeth Kübler-Ross has helped counselors heal angry people who blame God. This passage concerning anger and death may help those grappling with anger and scrupulosity:

Many chaplains are very good as long as the patient displaces the anger onto the hospital administration, nurses, or other members of the helping profession. But as soon as the patient expresses anger at God, they have the need to put the brakes on. I think it is very important that patients are allowed to express their anger at God, and my answer to chaplain students is always, "Do you really think that you have to come to God's defense? I think God can take it. He is bigger than that." (Kübler-Ross 1981, 43)

Effective therapists encourage people with Scrup/OCD to experience their flow of thoughts. Behavioral therapists suggest that doing so causes the sufferer to become *habituated*. As people living near airports or expressways become used to these annoyances, persons with Scrup/OCD can quell their anguish. They learn that their obsessive thoughts diminish when they prevent themselves from giving in to compulsive behaviors that only temporarily ease their anxiety.

• *Things that bother others pass them by.* Scrup/OCD produces slight benefits. If one is absorbed in worries about silly sins, real life worries lose their power. For some, physical illness, danger, economic problems, or draining social conditions evoke smaller measures of anxiety. One study during World War II highlights this. Anxious and neurotic soldiers expressed bravery and valor under fire. Their internal fears scared them more than the enemy.

• *They fear risks.* People with Scrup/OCD create rituals. These differ from official rituals of their religion and often have a magical quality. For instance, by saying a rosary twice they believe God will spare them from sickness. By reciting ten Hail Marys, they feel they can control their anger toward their aged mother who makes daily demands from the nursing home. By going to church every day and three times on weekends, they hope to garner prosperity.

Unfortunately these rituals rob them of a balanced life. Those afflicted turn down social invitations because they have to make that third Mass on Sunday. They reject a job promotion that involves traveling because it will disrupt their worship schedule. In biblical language, they create a Sabbath whom they serve. This locks them out of life's surprises.

• *Numbers are magic.* People with compulsive behaviors often use numbers as ways to regulate their lives. Freud recognized this, and compulsive people of all faiths have proven this throughout history. God gave Moses Ten Commandments. Catholics learned to count their sins before confession. Some psychologists go even further and think they can apply numbers to all behavior.

One man wrote: "I must complete a set formula of prayers. I can't talk to anyone until I've finished." I recently saw one man who felt compelled to crack his knuckles five times, but only after he cracked his toes five times. If he didn't do this the right way, he started over. St. Catherine prided herself on eating five orange seeds a day and nothing else. This signified the five wounds of Christ. As we shall learn in chapter 5, "Scrupulosity and Women," many women combine numbers, eating compulsions, and scrupulosity.

• *Sometimes they explode.* For a good deal of time most people with Scrup/OCD keep their temper in check. But this is hard work, and sometimes they lose it and become very angry. They may shout or yell. Situations of unfairness or people who block their rituals evoke rage. Friends express surprise, but family members are familiar with the pattern.

In severe cases, family members may unknowingly prevent rituals and anger follows. These are difficult situations, even for therapists. Behavior therapy that uncovers rituals and requires normality helps bring the family together.[14]

• *Their own feelings puzzle them.* Because they're afraid that feelings involving sin might appear at any moment, people with Scrup/OCD push away their own feelings. They may succeed in temporarily hiding irritations, resentments, or other uncharitable thoughts. Sadly, they also banish feelings of vulnerability, courage, and strong desires to love and be loved.

Psychodynamic therapies offer an understanding of this that behavior therapists haven't matched. Leon Salzman said that expressing vulnerability in the need for love is the key issue in helping people with OCD. He believes that developing security contributes to diminishing rituals. On the basis of the strong expressions of loneliness throughout the Scrup/OCD sample, I agree with Salzman.

In the past decade, psychiatrists and others have reported the presence of "alexithymia" in a variety of conditions. "Alexithymia" means unawareness of feelings. This word describes many sufferers of Scrup/OCD.[15]

• *They are trustworthy.* In most cases people with Scrup/OCD are true to their code of conduct. They keep confidences, pay their taxes, treat others fairly, and refrain from meanness or manipulation. The chapter on successful people and scrupulosity provides examples. In history, penitents loved and trusted St. Veronica Guliani and St. Alphonsus because they were trustworthy.

• *They look wimpy, but they're just waffling.* People underestimate the strength of those with Scrup/OCD. Because they ponder what to do, they may come across to others as weak or ineffective. In reality they're struggling with a thousand issues that they must resolve before they act. Once they make up their mind, they're capable of taking strong stands.

• *Sometimes they need clear direction.* In the chapters on the history of scrupulosity, we note that people with Scrup/OCD who changed history themselves required direction. Trusted confessors provided relief from scruples. The confessor's identity may have disappeared or become hidden, but the decisive and creative contributions by the Scrup/OCD sufferer live on. Many times the confessor ordered the scrupulous person to stop rituals, and this edict provided the necessary clarity.

For example, Martin Luther worried continuously about whether he did and said everything right during Mass. Millions of Catholic priests throughout history have said Mass without trepidation. Luther's long-distance correspondence with Dr. John von Staupitz, his trusted advisor, eased his judgmental fears. Luther's brilliance and insights on God's grace and love motivate ecumenical efforts into the twenty-first century. We forget Dr. Staupitz, yet he calmed Luther so Luther could think clearly. This reminds me of the song line, "You were the wind beneath my wings." Perhaps pastoral workers and therapists will recognize that they too played similar roles with their clients.

One reason for the success of behavior therapy with OCD is the directive and authoritative therapist. The therapist directs the patient to face fears and avoid rituals. In doing so, the patient learns to wait out and overcome terror and anxiety. Talk therapists who don't specialize in behavior therapy recognize that they must provide active direction in addition to empathy.

Many respondents in the survey noted that a spouse helped in times of indecision. However, research suggests caution. The literature on OCD suggests that requests for reassurance drain and alienate family members. This can be a difficult area in which to find balance for sufferer, counselor, and family member.

• *Some turn to alcohol.* Survey respondents expressed in myriad ways a desire to blot out or stop their thoughts. Some chose alcohol to help do this. OCD researchers recognize the risk of alcohol abuse or minor tranquilizer abuse in persons with OCD. But the temporary payoff is destroyed by addiction.[16]

• *Reading and thinking soothe and torture.* Some sufferers of Scrup/OCD become nervous or obsessed when reading or hearing certain scripture passages. These evoke doubts and fears. One man said that going to Mass made him feel "nutso." He reported that he got the bishop's dispensation so he could avoid church altogether. This example is extreme.

In the opposite vein, Scrup/OCD sufferers acknowledge the power of words and language to soothe temporarily or even heal. Scores of them wrote gratefully about the Scrupulous Anonymous newsletter. They said that reviewing these positive writings helped them when obsessing. For many, accounts of a loving and trustworthy God throughout salvation history provide therapy.

For people with OCD in general, Freud noted the importance of language.[17] As thoughts take on a real quality, language becomes tangible.

• *Sexuality frightens them.* Countless survey respondents grappled with sexual thoughts and feelings. They confuse thinking and feeling with sinning. They take St. Luke literally: "Anyone who looks at a woman with lust has committed adultery in his heart." The emerging sexuality of adolescence tortured many respondents. They felt constantly in a state of mortal sin. Many reported marital problems due to their fear or guilt over sexuality. Although Andrew Greeley has reported that Catholic couples express satisfaction with their sexual lives, for people with scrupulosity, sexuality continues to be a struggle.

One woman spoke for many survey respondents in describing her guilt over masturbation:

I have not described the sin that worries me the most. It is masturbation. I have sinned this way since a teenager. I've continued throughout my marriage. I looked for Catholic

*books that would give information but did not find any. All
I have is a strict list of sins in a prayer book. Once Ann Lan-
ders said that the church changed its position on this subject.
I remain confused.*

For this respondent and others who worry about this issue, the
Catechism of the Catholic Church provides reassurance. Habit,
anxiety, and immaturity lessen or negate sinfulness. The catechism
states:

To form an equitable judgment about the subject's moral responsibility and to guide pastoral action, one must take into
account the affective immaturity, force of acquired habit,
conditions of anxiety, or other psychological or social factors
that lessen or extenuate moral culpability.[18]

Behavioral therapists often help scrupulous people become
more comfortable with sexual issues. Dr. Edna Foa successfully
treated one man obsessed by the penis of Jesus Christ (Interview with Dr. Edna Foa, December 3, 1995). She helped him
accept the thoughts and eventually they faded. Behavioral and
talk therapies share common features: behaviorists help people
habituate to troubling images; effective talk therapists, by being nonjudgmental and compassionate, create a climate where
systematic desensitization and habituation can take place.

Several respondents feared that homosexual thoughts defined them as homosexual. Dr. Fred Penzel states, "As obsessive
thoughts go this type is probably more common than most people
realize. Sufferers find them extremely difficult to reveal or discuss,
due to the obvious embarrassment they feel. They live in isolation and shame as a result" (Penzel 1995). Dr. Penzel presents
approaches to help people face and build tolerance for these
thoughts.

• *Sometimes they get so fed up they sin or act out in extreme
ways.* Scrupulosity is like water torture. The constant dripping
wears down even the strongest. When this happens some sufferers rebel. They commit real mortal sins. They get drunk and
don't care. This provides short-term diversion, but they feel worse
afterward. One respondent offered words of encouragement to
others in this situation: "Having sinned mortally, now I know
how scruples differ. I can tell the difference."

Cardinal O'Connor suggests that scrupulosity can wear down the sufferer:

> People who feel impossibly frustrated and feel that what they are doing or what they are thinking or what they are experiencing is beyond their control, just say, "Well, the heck with it, I'm going to throw it all overboard. Instead of attempting to be a celibate, for example, I'm going to visit every prostitute I can visit."

This recalls St. Augustine's life. He recognized that a sinful life left him unfulfilled. However, instead of developing scrupulosity, he became remorseful. Cardinal O'Connor stated: "St. Augustine constitutes a one-man control group. He was a blackguard of a sinner but he was able to know true compunction, true sorrow, and had no difficulty with scrupulosity thereafter. He is a remarkable man. And extraordinarily, extraordinarily valorous" (Interview with John Cardinal O'Connor, January 23, 1996).

• *They fear losing control.* Fears of going crazy, killing others, and committing sexual offenses, blasphemy, or other atrocities bedevil the scrupulous. To protect themselves they create magical rituals. they think that cleaning the sink a certain way, saying prayers a certain way, or repeating certain actions keep them in control. A key goal of any therapy is to empower patients to accept these thoughts. By doing so, the thoughts lose their power. The person learns to respond to life flexibly.

Freud encouraged OCD sufferers by noting that they never act out their troubling thoughts — those that have a peculiar or bizarre nature. But as mentioned before, sometimes they become so disheartened by their constant scrupulosity that they may commit ordinary mortal sins as a form of relief.

• *Sometimes they feel like wound-up clocks.* People with Scrup/OCD plan carefully. Their lists fill paper as well as their consciousness. They must complete their listed activities precisely, which wearies them. One respondent stated: "Scrupulosity is compulsiveness. It's perfectionism. Scrupulosity is the inability to let life happen. It gets me very depressed. I work myself up to frenzy levels. I feel desperate, helpless, and alone."

• *It started in childhood.* One respondent wrote me a personal note: "By doing this project, you are tapping into a volcano of personal histories." Only a few survey respondents noted the beginning of Scrup/OCD in adulthood. In each case, this followed the death of a loved one. It is unclear why death or severe separation can be the catalyst evoking the emergence of scrupulous behaviors.

Most survey respondents worried as children. Early in life they ritualized. In fact, obsessive compulsive behaviors exist more commonly in children than adults, although most children outgrow these rituals. One respondent stated:

I grew up in a painful environment. I found ways to make myself happy. There was always underlying pain. My father is an alcoholic, a miserable one. When he drank, he argued and preached. He was right and you were wrong. When sober, he withdrew from everyone. You could never please him. I know my view of God probably came from this. My mother is narrow-minded, controls others, and acts like a martyr. Nothing I did was good enough to make my parents happy. I never knew what they expected of me.

• *"Te va a castigar Dios."* A man who healed his alcohol and scrupulosity problems stated:

My father used harsh words for discipline. My mother stripped us naked and beat us with a belt. When she berated us verbally, I remember her saying: "Te va a castigar Dios." This means, "God is going to punish you."

• *They always worry.* One respondent stated:

I'm always worrying. I look to worry. I anticipate disaster. My mind is rarely quiet and at peace. When I try harder to be good, scrupulosity intensifies. I get mad at myself. I fear that God is always mad at me.

• *They worry about leaving their germs on the toilet seat.* One respondent, displaying quick wit, stated:

I figured out how to tell the difference between plain OCD and scrupulosity. People with plain OCD worry about getting germs from other people. People with scrupulosity are afraid they will infect others with their germs. I know it's silly, but I carry around several handy wipes to protect others.

• *It eases but doesn't disappear.* Few survey respondents were cured. Even the most optimistic behavior therapists express caution. Traditional psychiatric thinking states that OCD waxes and wanes throughout a lifetime. Nevertheless, people with Scrup/OCD can select from many helpful resources, approaches unknown in years past. Solidarity with other sufferers provides further hopefulness.

Realistically, sufferers of Scrup/OCD can expect periods of relative peace but also times of increased symptoms. Bishop Howard Hubbard offers encouragement on this issue in chapter 14, "The Lilies of the Field."

• *They surprise themselves.* You may know someone with a bridge phobia. In the Hudson Valley where I live there are a number of long bridges. One has short guard rails, and this bridge terrorizes people with phobias. The terror that Scrup/OCD causes is similar to bridge phobia. Therapists recognize a puzzling aspect concerning bridge phobias and other phobias as well. In times of emergency, phobias disappear. There are accounts of women with bridge phobia who needed to take their child to a hospital. The hospital was across the river. Motivated by love of their child, they successfully crossed the bridge.

When people with Scrup/OCD face their fears, similar surprises occur. They abandon rituals for involvement in living and relationships with people. A positive spiral emerges, reported by behaviorists in their case studies. Some patients who develop lists of feared situations discover they can comfortably handle the most distressing situations earlier than they or their therapist imagined.

• *They are compassionate.* Perhaps this is a near universal quality of people with Scrup/OCD. They worry about others. They worry about the feelings of others. They feel the pain of other people. They make allowances for the sufferings of others because they know how hard life can be. Historical figures suffering from Scrup/OCD radiated empathy and compassion.

• *They would like to fall in love with the Lord.* In one of Solzhenitsyn's novels, someone suggests to Ivan Denisovitch, "Your soul wants to love the Lord. Why don't you allow it freedom?" (see Psalm 63, p. 179 below). Many with Scrup/OCD feel a similar longing, an inclination hard to describe. They step on their own feet as they try to fulfill that longing.

Talk therapists can help articulate these feelings. For some, Scrup/OCD symptoms can represent misplaced fears, misperceived terrors. They serve as helpful defenses designed to combat real trauma or abuse. These feelings cause distrust and fear of parental figures. As a result, such persons fear adult intimacy. In his book *The Future of an Illusion*, Freud said that images of God are projections. By this he meant that we apply to the Deity feelings from our own personal background.

Using Freud's own reasoning, the development of this thinking proceeds in a way he would not envision. Because of harsh images of parenting, people with Scrup/OCD fear or otherwise hold back from relating to God. I know that many therapists would think that removing religious thinking increases mental health, but several respondents assert the opposite. As their scrupulosity diminished — through drugs or therapy or a combination — they reported greater peace, healthy spirituality, and an awareness of love for rather than fear of the Lord.

• *They worry and they wash.* Judith Rapoport made the public aware of OCD with her book *The Boy Who Couldn't Stop Washing*. One respondent, retired from the accounting field, stated:

> *I'm afraid to touch door knobs, light switches, or anything connected with my elimination processes. I worry that I touched or might have touched the elimination processes of sinners. So I wash my hands and other articles excessively. I worry about sexual thoughts I have about men other than my husband, especially Jesus.*

One female respondent noted:

> *I am constantly washing my hands. I wash door knobs and even the bottom of my shoes. My fear is that I am never clean enough. I am not clean enough to go to church. I have been miserable for over forty years.*

• *They doubt.* One respondent stated:

> *I experienced crippling indecision in both large and small matters. I exaggerate the seriousness of my mistakes. Depression and hate fill my life.*

• *They waste years of time.* Time spent on rituals or twisted thinking is lost time. Especially when they become older, people with Scrup/OCD lament the misspent time, the wasted years. This evokes sadness and grief. Persons with OCD experience similar anguish (Rapoport 1990).

• *They worry their children will get it.* Recent professional writings have referred to biochemical and possible genetic causes of OCD, prompting many OCD sufferers to worry about passing it to their children. As yet, scientists offer no certain conclusions. Many persons with Scrup/OCD make every effort not to encourage these behaviors in their children. St. Alphonsus serves to inspire. Although afflicted with scrupulosity, he encouraged church practices emphasizing healthy spirituality.

• *They would trade it for a physical illness.* Many readers of this book who lack experience of Scrup/OCD may doubt this assertion. Unbelievable as it sounds, several survey respondents said they thought their scrupulosity was worse than cancer. How can this be?

An anecdote from the beginning of my career may help us to understand this better. I was working in a psychiatric hospital. As I was walking out of a draining meeting with a patient and his family, the medical director, an experienced psychiatrist, said to me, "Mental illness can be worse than cancer." Several weeks later, I visited a friend who was a patient at Sloane-Kettering Hospital. My friend suffered in the terminal stage of leukemia. As I went toward his room, I noticed many signs of support for patients in this hospital. Relatives flew in from all over the country to express love and encouragement. Many showed physical affection. Families and friends pulled together. Florists delivered beautiful flowers. There were many clergy available. This contrasted with the scene at the psychiatric hospital, where there were few visitors, little support, and much shame and embarrassment. With greater understanding of mental health problems, I hope sufferers will feel united and not isolated from others.

• *Others tire of their worrying.* People close to sufferers of Scrup/OCD may be worn down by their worries or rituals. In the past, some priests even hoped to avoid their confessions. In a derogatory manner, they referred to them as "scrups." One respondent noted: "How does the average priest feel about the scrupulous? We bug some of them. To me everything is serious. I am not a fun person and I hate it."

Successful treatment of the person with severe Scrup/OCD includes working with family members. The therapist shows them how to keep normal family routines running smoothly. Family members may have learned to give in to keep the peace, but this is not helpful and breeds resentments.

• *Their untapped courage runs deep.* Their fight against imaginary demons inoculates them for big battles.

• *Some harness the energy.* Spending hours on meaningless rituals or fears is wasteful or silly. Applying energy and carefully completing real life plans is the core of success. Many survey respondents described how their scrupulosity helped them at work.

• *They laugh nervously, but need to experience real humor.* People with Scrup/OCD titter and smirk. Full laughter eludes them. They take themselves too seriously and laugh out of embarrassment rather than joy. Father O'Flaherty thought that the presence of true laughter indicates improvement and even cure.

• *Life is a veil of tears.* Sixty-seven percent of respondents said that significant depression accompanied their scrupulosity. This parallels professional findings on OCD.[19] Many make their own misery, entangling themselves in peculiar rituals. They immerse themselves in negative thinking. Chapter 13 suggests that cognitive therapy approaches to depression can be used to treat Scrup/OCD as well. One respondent wrote:

> *I have given up the prospect of ever receiving Sacraments again. I pray for a speedy death every day. I have serious financial problems. I feel too cowardly and unloving for the Christian life. I have only been to Communion about eight times between the ages of fourteen and forty-four.*

• *Reality creates some worries.* For some people with scrupulosity, their worries merge with real-life troubles. One respondent stated:

> *My father died when I was five years old. My mother remarried. I didn't like my stepfather. When my mother got angry at me she said, "You're going to be the cause of my death." When I stayed over with friends I was afraid she would die*

while I was gone. I use to look in the obituaries to see if her name was there.

• *Scrup/OCD embarrasses them.* It has taken sufferers of OCD longer to "come out of the closet" than people with other disorders. For example, most of us understand depression. Alcoholism is an extreme of normal drinking. Because of the strange and peculiar nature of many OCD symptoms, sufferers hesitate to acknowledge them. I have even heard of cases of people in therapy for several years who never mentioned their OCD to their therapist. Instead, they talked about the many problems of their life. People with OCD or Scrup/OCD frequently think others will judge them as weird or crazy. Because of this, they guard their secret emotional life.

We live in an age that deemphasizes or disrespects traditional religious beliefs. As a group, mental health professionals lack openness to religious experience. Some brand even normal religious practices as sick. Because people with Scrup/OCD know this, is it any wonder that they remain secretive?

Historical research suggests that the increased religiosity of past ages made Scrup/OCD easier to acknowledge. Unfortunately, our ancestors lacked modern therapy. Increased openness about Scrup/OCD will link sufferers with help and hope.

• *Freud's cases demonstrate kinship with contemporary sufferers of Scrup/OCD.* The Rat Man experienced strong mixed feelings toward many childhood events. Love and hatred existed in uneasy co-existence. Freud believed symptoms of Scrup/OCD diverted his patient from his painful conflicts. Freud stated:

The conflict between love and hatred showed itself in our patient by other signs as well. At the time of the revival of his piety he used to make up prayers for himself, which took up more and more time and eventually lasted for an hour and a half. The reason for this was that he found, like an inverted Balaam, that something always inserted itself into his pious phrases and turned them into their opposite. For instance, if he said, "May God protect him," an evil spirit would hurriedly insinuate a "not." On one such occasion the idea occurred to him of cursing instead, for in that case, he thought, the contrary words would be sure to creep in.... In the end he found his way out of his embarrassment by giving

up the prayers and replacing them by a short formula con-
cocted out of the initial letters or syllables of various prayers.
He then recited this formula so quickly that nothing could
slip into it. (Freud 1963, 35–36)

The Wolf Man, another famous Freud patient, expressed Scrup/
OCD in this manner:

He related how during a long period he was very pious. Before he went to sleep he was obliged to pray for a long time
and to make an endless series of signs of the cross. In the
evening, too, he use to make the round of all the holy pic-
tures that hung in the room, taking a chair with him, upon
which he climbed, and used to kiss each of them devoutly.
There was another fact that was utterly inconsistent with
this pious ceremonial — but perhaps it was, nevertheless,
quite consistent with it — for he recollected some blasphemous thoughts which used to come into his head like an
inspiration from the devil. He was obliged to think "God —
swine." (Freud 1963, 35–36)

Another part of the Wolf Man's rituals was described in this way:

A part of the pious ritual by means of which he eventually
atoned for the blasphemies was the command to breathe in
a ceremonious manner under certain conditions. Each time
he made the sign of the cross he was obliged to breathe in
deeply or to exhale forcibly. In his native tongue "breathe"
is the same word as "spirit," so that here the Holy Ghost
came in. He was obliged to breathe in the Holy Spirit or
to breathe out the evil spirits which he had heard and read
about. (Freud 1963, 225)

• *From understanding to help and hope.* Upcoming chapters
offer more information on scrupulosity, and move from what it
has been in the past, to how it is experienced today, to what it
could be like in the future.

Chapter 3

AUGUSTINUS GEMELLI

According to my research, the first book on scrupulosity from a scientific perspective was *De Scrupulis Psychopathologiae Specimen in Usum Confessariorum,* written by Augustinus Gemelli.[20] As a young man Gemelli, a fervent socialist, lost his faith in purely scientific philosophy and became a Franciscan priest, medical doctor, and then psychiatrist. While still a young priest and doctor, he wrote his work on scrupulosity, which appeared in print as the world prepared to fight World War I. After writing the book, Gemelli's career flourished. He displayed leadership talents, founding the Catholic University of Florence and a worldwide association of Catholic universities. He displayed a brilliant legal mind in numerous works on canon law. Modern canon lawyers continue to refer to his landmark "Gemelli case," as a result of which the Catholic Church became more liberal in granting marriage annulments.[21]

Gemelli wrote his first book in his native Italian language (Gemelli 1913), and a Latin translation appeared in 1913. It was part of a series of books for priests meant to bring them up to date on medical and psychiatric questions. For that era, it was a revolutionary idea.

Affirming the importance of Gemelli's book was a preface by Désiré Joseph Cardinal Mercier of Belgium. Cardinal Mercier became one of the greatest twentieth-century cardinals; his courageous stand against the Nazis inspires us even today.

Gemelli designed his book to be a *vade mecum* — a book for priests to carry. Gemelli wanted priests to understand scrupulosity from a scientific point of view and to be able to make practical interventions. Gemelli recognized the penchant of scrupulous people for worrying about sin and forgiveness. He called this their "mania for expiation." He gave priests examples of ways to ques-

36

tion the penitent about sins. He emphasized that priests needed to reinforce the validity of absolution.

Gemelli noted that attention problems and even motor tics occurred among people with obsessive compulsive disorder and scrupulosity. This observation lay dormant, unexplored by other scientific researchers until the 1980s. At this time, psychiatric researchers hypothesized a continuum involving obsessive compulsive disorder, attention deficit disorder, and Tourette's syndrome. Current researchers examine this relationship.

Gemelli characterized scrupulous people as suffering from "the stigmata of the scrupulous state." In the Latin version of his book, he uses the original Italian to explain the anguish of the scrupulous person. *Sentimente incompleti* can be translated as "sense of difficulty, ineptitude, and imperfect perception." He coined other phrases that skillfully depict the thinking of people with Scrup/OCD: "indolence, fluctuations of the soul, retardation of action, absence of a position, inertia, mental eclipse, and perturbations of attention span" (Gemelli 1913). These terms aptly describe the thinking of many survey respondents cited in the following chapters.

One theme of this book is the link between scrupulosity and depression. Gemelli recognized the sense of melancholy that accompanies scrupulosity. He emphasized that scrupulous people display a great need to receive love. He recognized that they fear "terrors of solitude."

Like Freud, Gemelli expressed humility about the capacity of psychiatric science during his time to understand fully the causes of scrupulosity. In fact, he emphasized that it was "impossible" to determine specific causes.

Gemelli used his own scientific data as well as several studies by others. He hypothesized that scrupulosity was a constitutional illness that is hereditary.

He recognized a *spirite bizarre,* that "bizarre spirits" run in families. He quoted a study by Pitires and Regis, showing out of a hundred scrupulous people, 24 percent had a mother who was scrupulous, 5 percent had a father who was scrupulous, and 10 percent had close family members who were scrupulous (Pitires and Regis 1908, cited by Gemelli 1914).

The current study corroborates these figures. In the Scrupulous Anonymous survey 25 percent reported having a mother who experienced scrupulosity, 7 percent said that other family members were scrupulous, and 12 percent said that their father was scrupulous. These figures are remarkably similar to data presented by Gemelli over eighty years ago.

Dr. Jack Sherman, a noted geneticist, reviewed the data presented by Gemelli as well as the data assembled in our research. Sherman suggested that scrupulosity displays a family pattern consistent with a multifactorial genetic inheritance (discussed in greater length in chapter 11), a scientific insight that provides a great deal of hope for the effectiveness of therapies. As Thompson and Thompson in *Genetics in Medicine,* 5th ed., state with reference to multifactorial genes: "The effect of environment on their expression appears to be much greater than for other genetic diseases" (Thompson, McInnes, and Willard 1991).

Gemelli devoted the latter third of his book to possible results of scrupulosity (prognosis) and ways of treating it. "It is clear and I do recognize, that this counsel I have in mind must be done by experienced people," Gemelli stated. "Total healing may be evasive when depression is accidental. Where depression is constitutional, it may be more difficult to treat."

Gemelli asserted that the cure for scrupulosity would come from combining science and the confessional. Gemelli observed that the noted psychoanalyst Janet himself wrote "that priests understood and knew the illness of scrupulosity way before medical professionals."

Biological treatments for scrupulosity intrigued Gemelli, but he lacked enthusiasm that they would lead to a cure. The physical therapies of early twentieth-century psychiatry included sedatives, tonics, hydrotherapy, and hypnotism. Gemelli believed that psychotherapy held the most promise in treating scrupulosity.

Gemelli displayed kinship with behavior therapists in stating the importance of deciding to battle scrupulosity: "A person must be able to say '*Volo,*' I will."

Gemelli noted that many scrupulous people display a quality he called *surmenage,* an overmanaging or overcontrolling of one's life. Perhaps the contemporary equivalent of sufferers of *surmenage* is booked-up people who write in their day timer appointment books with five colors of ink.

Gemelli suggested that scrupulous people need to learn to live a balanced life: "It is preferred to have varied and tranquil work from which to derive pleasure and utility. This remakes the mind and indirectly the body."

Gemelli's words touched me. He represents a burst of study devoted to scrupulosity in the early part of the twentieth century involving the collection of scientific data. Gemelli longed for a cure for scrupulosity, but he was stymied because psychiatry and psychology were in their infancy. World War I diverted everyone's attention to more urgent matters. Gemelli's descriptive insights about scrupulosity are a treasure, and the fact that his work is virtually unknown saddens me. Books such as Judith Rapoport's *The Boy Who Couldn't Stop Washing* provide a good description of obsessive compulsive disorder — insights helpful to sufferers of Scrup/OCD. However, current researchers should recognize that there is earlier important scientific material on scrupulosity and obsessive compulsive disorder, pertinent insights from nearly a century ago.

How would Gemelli view current developments in treating scrupulosity and obsessive compulsive disorder? I think he would applaud advances made in medication. He would advocate further research into genetics and heredity. A man of action who knew the importance and the power of the human will, he would value the work of cognitive and behavior therapists. I don't think he would lose his enthusiasm for talk therapies. He would encourage healthy spirituality, as in the material suggested by Joseph Cardinal Bernardin in chapter 15. His knowledge of the entangled thinking and great suffering of people with Scrup/OCD would lead him to combine the best of all approaches to help heal the tremendous anguish caused by scrupulosity.

Chapter 4

MEN AND SCRUPULOSITY

Scrupulosity lurks among religious giants of the past five centuries. Some suffered from scrupulosity outright and wrote frankly about its healing. In order to treat his own scrupulosity St. Ignatius wrote the *Spiritual Exercises*. Martin Luther wrote theology: since God's grace rather than our own works saves us, we needn't fret about our sins. St. Alphonsus Liguori became the patron saint of religious counselors and confessors. George Fox, Quaker founder, desired pure religion; he instituted changes practiced today by the Society of Friends.

William James emerges in this discussion. Throughout his life, he doubted. Plagued by uncertainty, he yearned to believe. He sought to understand religion from the inside out. We still read his book *The Varieties of Religious Experience*, which explores how various people experienced their faiths (James 1982).[22] James distinguished between healthy-minded religion and religious sickness, which I try to do in this book also.

This chapter deals with the presence of Scrup/OCD in thinkers who influenced history. Like the survey respondents discussed in chapter 6, they led productive lives.[23]

St. Ignatius of Loyola

St. Ignatius is known for his great religious zeal and organizational ability. The Society of Jesus, or Jesuits, which he founded, have played a major role in church history over the past 450 years. In the United States today, the Jesuits run a highly regarded group of universities including Georgetown, Boston College, Loyola University of Chicago, and Fordham.

In the back of Ignatius's achievements lurked a nagging case of scrupulosity. Perhaps early life trauma contributed. His mother died after childbirth, and his father sent him into foster care. A blacksmith's wife raised him, and he played with her children. "We can assume that the combination of the loss of his mother and the exile from the castle of Loyola must have had great psychic impact on the infant who was to become the great saint and founder of the Society of Jesus" (Meissner 1992, 11). Ignatius converted to full Catholicism in a cave at Manresa, Spain, in 1522. Here he grappled with the demons of scrupulosity.

> At this time he had much to suffer from scruples. Although the general confession he had made at Montserrat had been entirely written out and made carefully enough, there still remained some things which from time to time he thought he had not confessed. This caused him a good deal of worry, for even though he had confessed it, his mind was never at rest. He began, therefore, to look for some spiritual man who would cure him of his scruples, but without success. Finally, a doctor of the cathedral church, a very spiritual man who preached there, told him one day in confession to write out all he could remember. He did so. But after confessing it his scruples returned, each time becoming more minute, so that he became quite upset, although he knew that these scruples were doing him much harm and that it would be good to be rid of them. (Meissner 1992, 74)

Ignatius found peace by writing out all the sins he felt he had committed. Much like the alcoholic who hits bottom, he became disgusted with himself. He resolved to forget his past sins, but despite this improvement, scruples returned at various times in the future. As was the case with other historical figures and people in our survey, one special person helped Ignatius. This unknown monastic priest "played a crucial and highly influential role" in healing Ignatius (Meissner 1992, 79).

The Spiritual Exercises of St. Ignatius

Although Ignatius wrote the *Spiritual Exercises* three hundred years before the appearance of behavioral psychologists, his ideas are similar to theirs.[24] He emphasizes journal writing and list-ing sins. He encourages substituting new habits for old ones and instructs us to use our imagination to imagine a loving God. He speaks of "battle" and "struggle," words that strike a chord in anyone with Scrup/OCD. As Cardinal O'Connor has stated: "Certainly the Ignatian Exercises and thirty-day retreat include a wealth of material" applicable to scrupulosity (Interview with John Cardinal O'Connor, January 23, 1996). Ignatius attributes his scrupulous thoughts to the Enemy, the Devil, a power resid-ing outside the soul. Modern-day sufferers, while not invoking the Dark Power, intuitively assert the foreign nature of OCD.[25] Doubts followed Ignatius throughout his life. His confessors helped him, and he often turned to a "trustworthy mentor for help in reaching decisions or clarifying uncertainties" (Meissner 1992, 79).

The Exercises can provide insight and help for Scrup/OCD, with some reservations. There is a danger that certain obsessive compulsive aspects of the Exercises could "hook" a person, for example, listing all sins by the hour. Many people with Scrup/OCD do this already. They mistake thoughts for acts and worry whether a thought or feeling was a slight sin or grave sin. Modern therapies of every school encourage people to accept the flow of inner thoughts and feelings. Feeling is not doing.

Ignatius recommended that people take his Exercises in a re-treat rather than by reading them. A wise spiritual director customizes the Exercises for each individual.

In the Spiritual Exercises meditations from the New Testament emphasize Christ's love and compassion. Like behavioral psychol-ogists, Ignatius recognized the power of imagery and encouraged visualizing details of the Gospel. He strove to make spirituality interesting and relevant (see also chapter 15). When this occurs, scruples diminish and stereotyped thinking breaks apart.

The Exercises have helped many people make life decisions regarding "states of life." Traditionally this involved deciding be-tween a religious and a lay state. Now many life choices are involved. People with scrupulosity waffle on decisions, and can benefit from the systematic approach provided by the Exercises. The Exercises encourage risk-taking and trust.

Father Vincent O'Flaherty and Curing Scruples

Father Vincent O'Flaherty, a modern Jesuit in the tradition of St. Ignatius, wrote his *How to Cure Scruples* as Vatican II evolved. His book provides gems of empathy and insight into the scrupulous mind, and his ideas are consistent with behavior therapy as well as the ideas of the Jesuit founder (O'Flaherty 1966).

O'Flaherty exudes optimism regarding scrupulosity but suggests the need for special training in dealing with it: "The care of the scrupulous is a speciality requiring specific preparation." Among the principles he discusses are the following:

1. Telling a person to "forget it" doesn't work. Effective helpers and compassionate family members recognize this.

2. Scrupulous people avoid healthy religious practice. This creates a vicious cycle. "A scrupulous person instinctively avoids churches, retreats, religious books, and pious organizations because they excite scruples."

3. Counselors find scrupulosity difficult to diagnose and other serious problems may coexist with scrupulosity. Chapter 10 looks at this closely.

4. Real guilt exists. Scrupulosity obstructs atonement when real issues are avoided because of fussing over scruples. Freud and O'Flaherty agree. Real guilt requires confrontation, behavior change, and atonement.

5. Life circumstances affect scrupulosity differently. For one person, divorce may relieve scrupulosity. For a lonely single, marriage may provide respite.

6. Scrupulosity can snare counselors. Some counselors enjoy talking about scruples, which may interfere with the work. O'Flaherty cautioned, "the counselee may be wealthy and the counselor may need the fat fee." Managed care evolved because of situations like this.

7. Writing out scruples can help in confronting them.[26]

8. Scrupulosity is selective. It may not affect a person in all life areas.

9. When scruples clear, counselees rediscover lost emotions. This also occurs in recovery from alcoholism.

10. O'Flaherty recommends "examining the whole course of a scruple." One scruple opens many doors. Edna Foa would agree.

11. Vivid distractions help divert people from scrupulosity.

12. Cure of scrupulosity doesn't resolve pain, illness, and trauma. "Anyone who wishes to be cured of scruples must be resigned to bear his share of the doubts and fears present by the will of God in the trials of his life."

13. Self-directed humor provides relief.

14. Groups can be helpful.

15. Healing requires reparation of damage to others.

> There is great diversity in the inconveniences which he imposes on his family, business associates, and friends. His edicts on behavior are not bellowed out from his throne of righteousness but are promulgated through grapevines in whispers. Thus, one employee will buzz the information to another, that the boss does not approve of chewing gum. At home, the family will wake up some morning to discover that the night light was turned off and from then on, henceforth and forever, under penalty of deprivation of approval, no night lights will ever burn again in that household.

St. Alphonsus Liguori

St. Alphonsus developed creative counseling approaches, relevant even today. He is the patron of confessors. He began life in a wealthy family and distinguished himself as a successful lawyer at a young age. He loved making up lists or guidelines. (People with Scrup/OCD will smile.) He held lawyers to high standards; his maxims included: no lawyer undertakes an unjust cause; lawyers study all evidence; when a lawyer through delay or negligence loses his case or injures his client, he is bound to make compensation; justice and probity accompany the lawyer as companions

(Benedictine Monks of St. Augustine's Abbey 1921; henceforth Benedictines).

Alphonsus preferred helping the poor and sick to practicing law. "He did all this with as much gentleness and care as if they had been his own brothers" (Benedictines 1921, 361). Law disillusioned him. He saw corruption and injustice and decided "a man's conscientiousness may lose him his case" (Benedictines 1921, 367). Against his wealthy family's wishes, he joined a religious order.

Despite his outward success, scrupulosity plagued Alphonsus throughout his life. But he trusted his confessor, Father Pagano: "My scruples often keep me in anguish; but my blind obedience to Father Pagano used to calm those interior storms" (Benedictines 1921, 368).

He made a list of resolutions to help him be a better priest, which enabled him to organize his actions and prevented him from getting lost in a sea of self-doubt. Alphonsus resolved:

1. Christians see me as a minister of reconciliation. I must always be in the state of grace and God's friendship.

2. I must always be a good role model.

3. I need courage to overcome my own problems.

4. I am a priest. It is my duty to inspire others with a love of virtue and glorify the Eternal Priest, Jesus. (Benedictines 1921, 376–79)

His devotion is contagious, as in this prayer.

> O my Lord, I am about to offer up Thy Blood for sinners and for myself, the most perverse and ungrateful of all. I am about to offer it to obtain from Thy mercy the graces of which I stand the most in need, and especially that of always celebrating worthily. And I ask not only to persevere in grace, but to grow continually in Thy love, so that I may ever accomplish not my will but Thine. Never permit me, O my sole and sovereign God, to be separated from Thee by a single mortal sin, or even to wrong Thee by a venial sin of full deliberation. (Benedictines 1921, 381)

Alphonsus required weekly confession because of his self-perceived sins.

Agitations of mind, doubts, and inquietudes so tormented
him as to become a veritable martyrdom. The pages of his
private diary enable us to follow the stages of the painful
road he had to travel — a road where he carried a cross so
heavy that he could scarcely have struggled on, had not his
steps been supported by the constant help of his director.
(Benedictines 1921, 384)

Because he suffered, he was able to help others replace doubt
with confidence because his own life required this. "He wished in
all points to find a means of escape from doubt, without trenching
on the rights of the law on the one hand, or sacrificing those of
liberty on the other" (Benedictines 1921, 386–87).

Alphonsus as counselor inspires any psychotherapist or pastoral worker:

His method in the confessional was as surprising as his
manner in the pulpit, for it was in striking contrast with
the rigorism which then reigned supreme. According to the
Jansenistic spirit of the age, the poor sinner was never sufficiently prepared to receive absolution for his sins, nor was
any penance sufficiently crushing to expiate them. Penitents
were thus driven away from a sacrament which for them had
ceased to be a sacrament of mercy. The young confessor had
been brought up among the partisans of this rigid school,
but he felt instinctively what his studies and experience were
to prove later on: that in the spiritual guidance of souls the
golden mean should be followed between the laxity which
never rouses the sinner from his vice, and the rigorism which
drives him to despair. Severe toward himself, but indulgent
toward others, Alphonsus received the greatest sinners with
kindness. "The more heavily a soul is enslaved by vice," he
used to say, "the more necessary it becomes to use gentleness
to free it from its chains." He listened patiently and tenderly
to the penitent, and at the end disposed him for receiving
absolution. As to the sacramental penance, instead of over-
loading his penitents with difficult penitential works, which
are often left undone, he used to impose simple exercises of
devotion, such as would turn the soul from sin and stimulate
its fervor. (Benedictines 1921, 389)

These words live on to inspire contemporary confessors and suffers of Scrup/OCD.

Martin Luther

Martin Luther suffered from Scrup/OCD. His own cure for them contributed to the Protestant Reformation. Martin Luther grew up in a comfortable German family. His father sent him to college, hoping his son would become a lawyer. Luther had two loves, partying and the library.

> One day — when he was in his twentieth year, and he had been at the university two years — while engaged as usual in glancing over the library manuscripts, he chanced to open an old volume, mouldy and cobwebbed. Attracted by its antique aspect, Luther read its title and found it to be a Latin Bible, the first he had ever seen. This he read and re-read with inexpressible and never-ceasing delight, mingled with some astonishment, for until then he had imagined that the fragments of Scripture contained in the various collects of the Roman ritual embraced the whole word of God. Thus in an obscure corner of a neglected library, locked up in the Latin text, was discovered to Martin Luther that book which he was so instrumental in restoring to its pristine dignity, purity, and authority, and which he did so much to popularize by that admirable German translation in which his countrymen still read the oracles of God. (Martyn 1866, 39; see also Gritsch 1983)

Another step toward priesthood occurred when one of Luther's close friends was killed. Later Luther was caught in a storm and vowed to become a monk if God spared him.

Luther lived in an Augustinian monastery, which sheltered him from the vices of sixteenth-century Catholicism. He wanted to write, but instead his superiors ordered him to clean and beg. Monastic duties obsessed Luther. No matter how he tried, he couldn't attain perfection. Doubts plagued him: "the dolorous mysteries of a life of abstinence and fanatic dreamings — the infinite hard fights that have been fought, noiselessly and unrecorded, in the monk's dark, narrow cell" (Martyn 1866, 53).

Like Ignatius and Alphonsus, Luther was blessed with a wise confessor. Dr. John von Staupitz encouraged Luther to meditate on the spirit of the law rather than microscopic infractions. "I frequently corresponded with Dr. Staupitz," Luther said.

> Once I wrote to him, "Oh my sins, my sins, my sins!" Whereunto he replied, "You would fain be without sin. You have no right sin, such as murdering of parents, blaspheming, adultery, and the like. Thou hadst better keep a register of right and true sins, that so thou mayest not afflict thyself about small matters. Remember that Christ came hither to pardon our sins." (Martyn 1866, 61)

Luther's symptoms became very severe and possibly included major depression, panic disorder, and bipolar disorder. Erik Erikson suggests that Luther grew up with a love/hate relationship with his parents. Teachers treated him brutally, which left scars, perhaps related to scrupulosity. Luther stated,

> One ought not to flog children too hard. My father once whipped me so that I ran away and felt ugly toward him until he was at pains to win me back. My parents kept me under very strict discipline, even to the point of making me timid. For the sake of a mere nut stolen from the kitchen supply, my mother beat me until blood flowed. By such strict discipline they finally forced me into the monastery. I once was whipped fifteen times one morning in school. (Gritsch 1983, 148)

Luther resolved his scrupulosity by creating a new theology. We don't earn heaven; God's grace saves us. Faith, not works, justifies us. Obsessive compulsive rituals don't win salvation.

New studies on Martin Luther's life suggest that anxieties continued to plague him, and he continued to have trouble with women for the rest of his life.

Erasmus

Erasmus also suffered from Scrup/OCD. Like many survey respondents and OCD sufferers, Erasmus feared germs and sickness. He demanded antiseptic conditions and insisted on clean hotel linens. He requested frequent changes in holy water and baptismal water in church. He didn't like kissing and feared syphilis (Huizinga 1957, 121).

Depression accompanied him throughout his life. He lacked happiness and coined a term, *putidulus,* meaning "the quality of never being content with himself." Erasmus hated his appearance. Even minor flaws drew self-criticism. He looked at a picture of another with envy and said, "If Erasmus still looked like that, he would take a wife at once" (Huizinga 1957, 121).

William James, the Founder of American Psychology

William James struggled throughout his life with doubt and depression, two companions of Scrup/OCD. He believed that "the best things are the eternal things" and devoted his life to studying religious experience.

James suffered from "near suicidal depression during 1868–1872, a period marked by acute acedia and its arrest by religious consolation" (Levinson 1981, 25). In his essay "Is Life Worth Living?" he addresses obsessive doubt, calling it "the questioning mania."

Like the 67 percent of survey respondents who noted significant depression, James battled depression. At one particularly despairing moment he noted:

> I awoke morning after morning with a horrible dread at the pit of my stomach, and with a sense of insecurity of life that I never felt before, and that I have never felt since. If I had not clung to scripture texts like "The eternal God is my refuge," etc., "Come unto me all ye that labor and are heavy laden," etc., "I am the resurrection and the life," etc. I think I should have grown really insane. (Levinson 1981, 26)

At this point in his life he unabashedly prayed, and it worked. Although he said later he felt silly praying, he always stopped at the Harvard Chapel on the way to work. He applied the James-Lange theory of emotions to himself: act and the feelings will follow.[27]

How can one discern healthy religious faith? James thought that if a person's beliefs brought good mental health, they were worthy of study. This recalls Jesus. "Master, how will we know if prophets we meet along the road are speaking the Truth." Jesus, in an empirical and pragmatic way, suggested "by their fruits you shall know them."

In his book *The Varieties of Religious Experience* James classified healthy and sick religious experiences. What is the healthy variety?

> In many persons, happiness is congenital and irreclaimable ...I mean those who, when unhappiness is offered or proposed to them, positively refuse to feel it, as if it were something mean and wrong.... St. Francis and his immediate disciples were, on the whole, of the company of spirits, of which there are of course infinite varieties.
>
> It is to be hoped that we all have some friend, perhaps more often feminine than masculine, and young than old, whose soul is of this sky-blue tint, whose affinities are rather with flowers and birds and all enchanting innocencies than with dark human passions, who can think no ill of man or God, and in whom religious gladness, being in possession from the outset, needs no deliverance from any antecedent burden. (James 1982, 79)

It may surprise Catholic readers that James believed Catholicism encouraged more positive religious feelings than Protestantism (James 1982, 80). He admired the "mind cure" school of thinking, which encouraged thinking positive thoughts to stimulate positive emotions. They were the ancestors of Norman Vincent Peale and cognitive therapy.

In a perceptive statement — and one extremely relevant to scrupulosity — James noted:

> On the whole, one is struck by a psychological similarity between the mind-cure movement and the Lutheran and Wesleyan movements. To the believer in moralism and works [the scrupulous person?] with his anxious query, "What shall I do to be saved?" Luther and Wesley replied: "You are saved now, if you would but believe it." And the mind-curers come with precisely similar words of emancipation " ... God is well, and so are you." (James 1982, 115)

In another statement that presages the last step of Twelve Step programs, James noted that

> a form of regeneration by relaxing, by letting go, psychologically indistinguishable from the Lutheran justification by faith and the Wesleyan acceptance of free grace, is within reach.... It is but giving your little private convulsive self a rest, and finding that a greater self is there. (James 1982, 115)

Another contribution of William James is his classification of religious experiences that are not helpful and productive into a category he called "the Sick Soul." He cited Goethe as someone who experienced this malady:

> "I will say nothing," writes Goethe in 1824, "against the course of my existence. But at bottom it has been nothing but pain and burden, and I can affirm that during the whole of my 75 years, I have not had four weeks of genuine well-being. It is but the perpetual rolling of a rock that must be raised up again forever." (James 1982, 128)

James hypothesized that some persons are born with a special sensitivity toward negativity. This is akin to genetic and biological theories of Scrup/OCD (James 1982, 127).

How can William James help scrupulous people? He provides hope, first, that doubt and despair do pass, as evidenced in his own life, and, second, that "right thinking" can help with scruples. This "right thinking" could include an awareness of the positive aspects of one's religious beliefs, as discussed in chapter 13. The Scrupulous Anonymous newsletter and related publications have been cited by survey respondents as being extremely helpful; such writings provide a positive interpretation of religious experience for people whose minds are apt to go off on sometimes peculiar tangents. Third, James gives us hope that cognitive therapy can provide assistance in healing the depression that accompanies scrupulosity and obsessive compulsive disorder.

How can William James assist therapists? First, therapists need to listen and learn about a person's religious tradition. Too many times therapists ignore the positive implications of a person's religious beliefs, or they simply don't understand. In the spirit of

William James, an empirical approach is suggested: when working with a scrupulous person, learn about the religious framework surrounding scrupulosity. Read books that explain the person's religious heritage; attain familiarity with inspired or sacred readings. In sum, be a "phenomenologist" and strive to understand the outlook of the scrupulous person from the inside. Second, therapists need to look for healthy spiritual aspects in a scrupulous person's life. Third, therapists need to be wary of trying to dissuade scrupulous persons from their faith.

Cardinal O'Connor, who holds graduate degrees in philosophy, with an emphasis on phenomenology, as well as clinical psychology and psychiatry, provided these reflections on the work of William James:

> I've had a good bit of counseling experience and a lot of teaching experience. I think it is helpful for any psychologist, and particularly a clinical psychologist, to have a foundation in philosophy. I would hope that the approaches and attitudes of William James might be considered with the seriousness that they deserve. But I think there was so much subjectivism in James's stream of consciousness approach to religion that readers should be aware of this bias on his part. I think that you must always distinguish between the subjective and objective. (Interview with John Cardinal O'Connor, January 23, 1996)

I hope that these themes from William James — optimistic and right thinking, looking for positive spirituality, and a scientific outlook — will inspire future progress in helping to heal scrupulosity/OCD.

Chapter 5

WOMEN AND SCRUPULOSITY

In the past fifteen years there has been increased recognition of the importance of studying female spirituality in its unique manifestations. Susan Muto, a recognized leader among those who study the spiritual lives of women, notes that scrupulosity and perfectionism are present in the lives of a number of prominent female mystics, including Julian of Norwich, Catherine of Siena, and Catherine of Genoa. These same traits occur with great frequency among contemporary women, as discussed later in this chapter.

In his book *Holy Anorexia* R. W. Bell suggests that obsessive compulsive disorder was often combined with eating disorders and perfectionism in prominent Catholic saints. The motive behind "holy anorexia," as Bell calls it, differs from contemporary anorexia.[28] Today, a slim and beautiful body brings attention; anorexia is an occupational hazard for stewardesses and models. In past Catholic cultures, the faithful viewed fasting as a virtue. Thinness and emaciation indicated discipline and holiness, and women who fast might obtain fame and adulation. Scrupulosity has evolved into a new form in women today, reaching beyond the church, but expressing a similar desire to please.

Scrupulosity in History

Veronica Guliani, born on December 27, 1660, is a Catholic saint who appears to have suffered from a combination of scrupulosity, obsessive compulsive disorder, and anorexia. Her confessors ordered her to keep a diary and she complied, so we know a great deal about her life and psychological states. She produced over twenty-two thousand handwritten pages, and people who knew her also wrote about her.

Like many people with Scrup/OCD, St. Veronica denied herself pleasure and even sought out pain. One day she punished herself by putting her fingers in the space between the front door and door jam of the house. A huge dog slammed the door shut, and one of her fingers bled profusely. A surgeon had to be called, who stitched the wound together.

As a child St. Veronica was feisty, outgoing, and generous. She displayed generosity. Once she was given a new pair of shoes, which she threw out a window to a beggar. She could be difficult:

> From her third autobiography and from testimony by nuns who lived with her many years and said that Veronica told them these things, we learned just what a brat she had been. When her sisters refused to leave their work to come to pray at her altars, she would go into a tantrum, take a cane, and start pounding on the furniture. When she was a teenager her father brought in rich and eligible young men to try to get her to date. She did not want to do this and she said to him harshly, "Do whatever you want, I will be a nun and you will see it is impossible to change me." (Bell 1985, 63)

Finally in 1677 her father gave permission to enter the convent. She reviewed her life with scrupulosity. For five years she repeatedly confessed the same sins. Her description of repeated confessions is similar to accounts provided by survey respondents. She developed anorexia, which lasted for five years. Her confessors and superiors ordered her to eat. Bell says,

> In evaluating the response by physicians, priests, and superiors to Veronica's anorexia we may recognize in the particulars of the late seventeenth-century religious beliefs and practices nothing less than a behavior modification program worthy of many a twentieth-century hospital. (Bell 1985, 82)

Increased responsibility offered the best therapy to St. Veronica. She was elected abbess in 1716, and, like St. Alphonsus, she distinguished herself by her compassion. She inspired others through her own example: she had been troubled but overcame her problems and discovered a healthy spirituality.

Simone Weil and Scrupulosity

From my vantage point, Simone Weil, a great woman of the twentieth century, appears to have suffered from the gnawing perfectionism that is part of scrupulosity. She experienced depression and despair, communicated to us through a theological vocabulary involving "the dark night of the soul." Like St. Alphonsus, she held herself accountable to almost inhuman standards but displayed bountiful empathy toward others. As a little girl and later, she frequently starved herself—a deprivation leading to her death at age thirty-four. A biographer wrote: "For those to whom religion means comfort and peace of mind, she brings the terrible reminder that Christ promised not peace but the sword, and that His own last words were a cry of absolute despair, the 'Eli, Eli lama sabachthani!' which is the true glory of Christianity" (Weil 1951, 5).

Simone Weil was born in 1909 into an agnostic family of Jewish heritage. Her parents' comfortable life clashed with her rigorous ideals. She gave up eating sugar at the age of five to support the French soldiers who were being gassed and shot along the German front. In middle childhood, her empathy for abused and poorly paid factory workers led her to give up wearing socks. At age fourteen she experienced suicidal urges and headaches that continued throughout her short life. At home, she felt inferior to her brother, "a mathematical prodigy, beside whose brilliance she felt stumbling and stupid" (Weil 1951, 15).

Simone Weil acted against poverty. She spent a year working at dirt wages in a French factory. Lung problems ended this venture. She traveled to Spain to support the Loyalists in the Spanish Civil War. This experience destroyed her faith in Marxism. As World War II approached she plunged into mystical experiences similar to those described by St. John of the Cross in *The Dark Night of the Soul*. She became absorbed with the passion of Christ and the meaning of the Our Father.

She avoided being baptized as a Christian. In 1942 her parents persuaded her to journey to America to regain her health. In 1943 she returned to England, where she tried desperately to work out a plan for reentering France. She refused to eat more than the rations allowed her countrymen in occupied France. Exhausted and weakened by fasting, she permitted herself to be brought to the country by well-meaning protectors. On August 24, 1943, she succeeded in dying, completing her life-long goal of "de-creation" (Weil 1951, 29).

Is this woman a saint? Did her psychological problems involving scrupulosity, depression, and an eating disorder help or hinder her holiness? Susan Muto has suggested that Simone Weil is a kindred spirit of Julian of Norwich and Catherine of Siena, and I hope others will develop this connection in greater detail (Interview with Susan Muto, February 13, 1996).

A New Scrupulosity

Kathleen Zraly is an eating disorders specialist, with a doctoral degree in psychology from Fordham University. She practices as an eating disorders counselor. We discussed scrupulosity's history. Does scrupulosity still exist? "Yes," Zraly stated.

> I think more so than any of us have any idea. Women continue to be socialized to be perfect, to carry the ball in all areas. Women with eating disorders display perfection that is a form of scrupulosity. They're never good enough. They're never pretty enough. Women are socialized that way, and the media reinforce this message.

Perhaps the church in the past exerted a force on women like today's broadcast and print media. Daily Mass required a lengthy fast before Communion. Priests not only proclaimed virtues, they evaluated them in confession. While women today pour over lists of calories, Catholic women in the past worried over lists of sins. The process and need to please remains the same. Zraly continued:

> In my practice I see women who struggle with superego issues. It's the inner voice that says "Tsk, tsk, you shouldn't do that." I think our clients are tremendously driven by guilt. They impose it on themselves or they feel that others place it on them.
>
> My clients are driven by guilt. This guilt is self-imposed or placed on them by society or family. I think that this type of outlook is a general moral scrupulosity rather than a specifically religious one.

Zraly emphasized the importance of positive spirituality for any women dealing with eating disorders, perfectionism, or related problems: "They need to develop a faith in themselves. They need to find something good about themselves and trust that events will work out."

Zraly herself discovered a new spirituality while living in a convent as she pursued doctoral studies in psychology at Fordham University. "I stayed at the motherhouse of the Immaculate Conception," Zraly said.

The sisters here taught me tremendously. We spent many hours at dinnertime talking about forgiveness therapy. Forgiveness frees women to face the future. In the last few years I found it very helpful to talk about and give my clients permission slips. I give them actual permission slips for forgiveness. Women need to forgive people who have hurt them but sometimes even more importantly they need to forgive themselves for falling short of the sometimes impossible standards and expectations they set for themselves.

A scrupulous and obsessive concern over physical appearance and attire entraps many women. This diverts energy from productive careers or rewarding relationships. Zraly stated:

The hair must be perfect, the nails flawless, the makeup elegant, every stitch ironed, and the shoes must match the dress. The handbag has to blend with everything. They underline appointment books in four colors. Their cars are immaculate. Their desks are spotless. Every doll or knickknack in their room is placed with precision.

They are scrupulous about wanting to become perfectly happy or wanting to be perfect at something like career, virtue, honesty, or integrity. It's all outside stuff. I see it as their way of saying to the world, "Who could question me? If everything on the outside that you see is flawless, who could ever question that anything inside might be askew?"

These women get away with it for a very long time, but after a while it catches up with them. And that's when their eating disorder or perfectionism or depression exacerbates and flares into a crisis.

Zraly offered these observations concerning the role of women students at the Culinary Institute of America, where she teaches:

Although women are supposed to be in the kitchen, 75 percent Culinary Industry students are men. And now all of a sudden these women aren't supposed to be in the kitchen and they're not supposed to be in the classroom either. This relates to perfectionism and scrupulosity. No matter how perfectly they try, they can't win.

Are there differences between men and women in the manner in which they worry and obsess?

Women worry about approval and recognition. I may get into trouble by saying this. The first thing many women do upon getting to the office is spending twenty minutes going around saying hello to everybody, standing at the coffee machine, touching base with everyone, and making sure everyone is okay. Women also worry but don't change the root cause of worry. They'll look at the gas gauge and worry about the tank getting empty. But instead of stopping, they drive on and keep worrying. Many men take control of the worry and stop and get gas. (Interview with Kathleen Zraly, January 10, 1996)

Susan Muto and Adrian van Kaam in their book *The Power of Appreciation* offer encouragement to anyone whose life is beset by scrupulosity or perfectionism: Obsessive Happiness Directives (OHDs)

are the culprits behind your thoughts of failure and disappointment.... By learning to redirect these urgings, by appraising them anew, you can prevent repeated falls from what you imagined to be the peak of happiness.... Spot and diffuse your OHD's, never believing that you are beyond the pale of transformation. Do not give in to the irrational spin that perpetuates a despondent life. (Muto and van Kaam 1993, 42)

As we have seen in some of the women featured in this chapter, traditional scrupulosity blended with rigorous adherence to a Catholic piety. The modern world evokes a new dimension of scrupulosity. While medieval and renaissance scrupulosity has faded or disappeared, a new scrupulosity of perfectionism beguiles modern women. Ideals previously put forth by the church are transformed into the ideals of modern society; the ideal parent, the ideal career person, the ideal community member. The psychological dynamic remains the same. It may be helpful for therapists and male clergy to recognize the unique presentation of Scrup/OCD in modern women.

Part Two

HOW IT IS

Part Two offers original data on the lives of people who suffer from scrupulosity and obsessive compulsive disorder. The chapters describe the continuum of severity of this disorder. Scrupulosity may exist as a self-contained component in the life of an otherwise psychologically healthy or successful person. In its most severe form it may co-exist with other traumatic psychological problems and require intensive therapy from a skilled and experienced mental health professional.

In chapters 6 through 9 I was inspired by the methodology of William James in his classic *The Varieties of Religious Experience*. I encourage all readers to become familiar with this masterful book.

Chapter 10 outlines a systematic way to determine the presence of scrupulosity, its severity, and its possible combination with other psychological problems. Mental health professionals and pastoral counselors may find this chapter illuminating.

Chapter 6

SUCCESSFUL PEOPLE AND SCRUPULOSITY

The following chapters present case studies similar to those in *The Varieties of Religious Experience* by William James. My goal is that persons with Scrup/OCD might feel kinship with others and that professionals gain increased awareness of Scrup/OCD and be stimulated to further research.[29] Scrup/OCD displays itself differently in each person. These narratives show its presence, from irritant to crippling condition.[30]

Scrupulosity presents itself as an irritant, quirk, or cross to bear. St. Ignatius viewed it as a problem in an otherwise healthy mind. Our survey validates this perception. Successful people, in a range of occupations, gave moving accounts which often remained hidden from family, friends, and co-workers. One professional wrote: "My scrupulous behavior is mainly mental. For me there is black and white, and few grey areas. I do not discuss this with my wife. It is between me and the creator."

Statistics from the survey suggest that Scrup/OCD and success can go together. For example, 50 percent of the respondents described their level of educational achievement as college graduate or professional. Even when Scrup/OCD symptoms were at their worst, 25 percent of respondents reported that they affected work only very little. Seventeen percent rated themselves as successful, and 50 percent rated themselves as devoted workers. Fifty-five percent perceived themselves as hardworking.

The etymological derivation of "scrupulous" suggests an original meaning as "a small amount." For people in this chapter, Scrup/OCD symptoms are small but powerful aspects of their lives. These stories suggest positive aspects of Scrup/OCD. Caring doctors and honest police captains demonstrate faith in society. Despite the suffering they inflict, Scrup/OCD symptoms can offer social benefits.

Physicians

One doctor has led a satisfying life for over sixty years. He wrote:

> I probably would be a candidate for a gold medal in the disease of scrupulosity. For many years I've suffered. I hope the many afflicted people can be helped. I remain anonymous, but will let you know that I am a successful physician, happily married, and father of four children. Praise God, my wife and I are new grandparents!
>
> My scrupulosity takes the form of excessive worry about moral issues that surround my family, my medical practice, and me. There is a spill of excessive worry about the legal-medical issues in my practice.
>
> For example, last night a call came to my answering service that I could not immediately answer. I had expected a call from a mother on a routine problem and I assumed this was the woman calling. When I arrived home, I returned the call. Much to my dismay I found it was from a father who reported his child having a seizure from a high fever. When I called the home the family had already left for parts unknown. I tried calling several emergency rooms, all to no avail. I was in a good mood until this call but then plunged into deep concern imagining all kinds of dire happenings. It ruined dinner for my wife and family because I was lost in worry. I made more calls later. It turned out that the child had a brief seizure. His father took him to a local doctor, and he was now fine. I know I should be concerned, but not worry so excessively. I forget God's love and protection of me and of the patients I care for. I do my best to be a compassionate and competent physician.

Most parents would be very grateful to have a doctor with a sense of scrupulosity. This physician's sense of caring for others outweighs his scrupulosity. He said, "My family corresponds with about twenty-five missionaries in Africa and India, and we help some poor families in town." His life reminds us of Erikson's concept of generativity (Erikson 1962). This man helps others and in doing so finds his life fulfilled.

This physician also expressed one troublesome issue reported by many respondents: birth control. He wrote:

> *For years, I functioned well. This preceded the confusion of Vatican II on the birth control issue. My wife and I during this period were just having children, adhering to church teaching and enjoying life. If priests had all rallied behind the teaching of* Humanae Vitae *my wife and I would have done fine. Such was not the case. I am sure that normal conjugal relations have much to do with lessening scrupulosity and the converse is also true.*

With a physician's perspective, this doctor concluded: "One person has diabetes, another heart problems, myself scrupulosity. I am not complaining."

Another physician, a practicing pediatrician, wrote:

> *Two major events in my life exacerbated my scrupulosity. I felt guilty on entering medical school because I had cheated on some college exams. I'm still guilty about that although I am a good pediatrician and have a loyal patient following. Also, I divorced my wife of twelve years six years ago. We had three children, and I am supporting them financially. I am planning to remarry but feel guilty about doing so, even though the church annulled my first marriage.*

For this doctor, Prozac helped a great deal. However, he noted, "Prozac has been very helpful but didn't cure the problem." Counseling by priests helped him. In addition, "accepting an authoritative role of the Catholic Church in my life helped me, and reading various publications. However, some material, even by the church, worsened my scruples. A commonsense approach to life, accepting my imperfections and failings, has provided peace."

A fifty-six-year-old female physician noted that, even when scrupulosity was at its worst, it affected her work only slightly. She reported: "I cannot receive Holy Communion unless I go to confession for at least three weeks prior. I suffer impure thoughts." This physician noted that confession has produced no change in her outlook. She said that a twelve-month stint in therapy helped a little.

College Teacher

A college teacher in Scotland wrote:

> *I have never really been able to trust in the love of God. I am afraid that God will pull the carpet out from under me. This stems from being taught as a child, "God is watching you." This made me bitter at times....Severe scruples ruined many years of my life. I suffered acute depression with nobody to turn to. In America you may think this strange. In my country we do not recognize mental illness. We see it as an American invention. My background was strict, and parents and church hammered religion into us. Everyone received a Ph.D. in Guilt. Everything you said, thought, or did, was sinful.*

For this professor, his emerging sexuality was particularly painful. While in America many young people were celebrating their sexual freedom, scrupulosity made coming of age for him an excruciating experience. He wrote:

> *I grew up with a distorted conscience on sex. What if this is a sin? What if it isn't? I flitted from book to book looking for answers. I found none. Confessions were fitful and an ordeal. Because of sexual exploration at an early age, which was no more than a response to anatomy, I suffered horrific guilt. The clergy stressed hell and damnation. My only rest from a tortured mind was sleep. I felt filthy and dirty and different. I believe that God had done his duty to punish me. Not once did a priest utter a kind word. I became bitter toward the clergy yet in complete awe of them. There is still venom in my heart after twenty years of suffering. Here were these men of God, unable or unwilling to help out. But one special priest rescued me from emotional condemnation. He rescued me from a maze.*

This man's life took a significant turn for the better:

> *I have led a fairly normal life in many ways, attending the university and teaching for eighteen years to date. Thank God I've had the sense not to subject my children to my upbringing. God forbid that they would ever suffer what I did. Perhaps in a more open society such as the U.S.A. this*

pain could have been prevented. Use my name. At this point in my life, I am indifferent to anonymity.

Like many respondents, he found some positive meaning in his suffering: "It has made me appreciate what happiness is. It had made me aware that money and position are meaningless if you lack peace of mind."

Police Captain

In an era of corrupt police and scandals, it is comforting to know that scrupulosity is present among our finest. It provides an antidote to unscrupulosity in our world. However, this same scrupulosity troubles the individual experiencing it. A fifty-two-year-old police captain stated: "I worry about what is sinful. I worry about sinful thoughts, discussions, or actions in my employment as a police captain and supervisor. I worry when I go to confession whether I might have omitted something." This person has not sought a therapist. He wrote that his confessor "helped by telling me to look toward the future." He reported that a spiritual director helped him by encouraging him to receive Communion frequently. When asked about any positive influence of scrupulosity, he stated: "Scrupulosity made me aware of how weak I am and totally dependent on God." It is especially interesting that this comment came from a man who described himself as "assertive" and who spends six hours weekly in physical training and weightlifting. Readers may share my relief that at least one such man leads police in America.

Naval Officer

A thirty-seven-year-old female naval officer reported: "I have recurrent thoughts which keep coming which I fear are sinful. This causes me to spend time analyzing them to decide if they're sinful, and it causes me anxiety and worry." This person has utilized several resources to control her scrupulosity. She discovered that therapy and medication have helped a great deal. Presently, she worries, however, "that I could pass this on to my children." On the positive side, she says scrupulosity has "kept me out of trouble and kept me humble."

Mathematician

One suspects that the attention to detail and the meticulousness accompanying scrupulosity could assist someone working with numbers. This is true for one forty-year-old male respondent. He said scrupulosity helped him in his "job as a mathematician, scientist, and engineer. I design computer systems that require a large degree of detailed planning and scrupulous thinking." He described himself as successful and hardworking but reported that his scrupulosity also involved "worry over moral matters." He said confession overwhelmed him in the past. Now, twenty years later, he confesses with more comfort. "I still worry about the outcome of projects I'm involved with at work and home," he said. He grew up in a troubled family. "I had a severely crippled mother and an alcoholic father and was the oldest child of three. I had to look out for various aspects of the family. I feared my father would be fired and unemployed." Reading books has been the main source of treatment. Unfortunately, he said, "Good confessors either died or were transferred."

Director of Religious Education

A religious education director reported: "Every time I do something I suspect is wrong, even if it isn't, I feel guilty and feel I'll get zapped." Therapy and confession helped considerably. Positively, her scrupulosity "made me continue to keep learning more about my religion and helped to deepen my faith."

Pharmacist

A fifty-two-year-old pharmacist wrote that he is "super worrisome that I cheated someone unknowingly. I fret that I may have charged the proper amount but gave the wrong change. I have an overriding desire to be perfect." He grew up "in a poor coal-mining family with one parent who was foreign born. I had three sisters. We lived in a small house with no indoor bathroom or furnace until I was fifteen or sixteen. We baked bread over a coal kitchen stove. We took a bath in a galvanized tub in the center of the kitchen once a week."

He noted that he has undergone a cycle of improvement and

regression "dozens of times." He reported a number of positive aspects of his scrupulosity:

It created a standard of excellence for my family, especially for my children. All achieved good working and educational status: excellent children physically, spiritually, and mentally! It has permitted me to experience faith in our Lord during times of trouble. I love to start and end the day in prayer and meditation. I love starting each day with the daily liturgy.

Forester

A forty-year-old forester reported that, because he works in nature, scrupulosity has not had a major impact on his career. Scrupulosity has taken the form of some obsession with perfectionism and a difficulty with intimate relationships. Scrupulosity at times has had a much more deleterious effect on his intimate relationships than his career. He provided further observations on his scrupulosity:

Sometime when I was in my late teens through my twenties I left the church. I experimented sexually and otherwise. My scrupulosity, especially regarding confession, returned when I went back to the sacraments. It's not as bad as before. Besides the spiritual expression of obsessive compulsive behavior in my scrupulosity, I've always been a perfectionist.

What has been most helpful, he reported, was a combination of spiritual direction and personal study. He said that readings by Dr. Conrad Baars on obsessive compulsive behavior "helped me understand how these 'pendulums' in behavior occur." He also noted that expression of sexuality within a context of values lessened the scrupulosity. He believes sexual acting out exacerbated the scrupulosity. He said,

Now I understand that my erratic sexual behavior stems from fear. I developed this in my teens. Worthlessness and poor self-image grew from not being able to control my legitimate and natural urges. Then I played this out through

promiscuity and dead-end relationships. In these ways I val-idated my guilty feelings. Scrupulosity helped me search a little for some real values to live by, as well as question my relation to God.

Nurse

A forty-nine-year-old nurse wrote:

Today my scrupulosity is just a tendency. However, it's like being alcoholic — one day at a time. Previously, I was always afraid of my doing wrong, especially in areas like possibly harming people or sexual thoughts and feelings. So I became paralyzed to act. Looking back I remember being scrupulous as a young school-age child. During most of my youth, I made frequent confessions. Some confessors were kind and helpful, some impatient.

At one point in life, in my late thirties, I sought help in confession. I had considered psychiatric help, but chose a priest because my concerns involved morality. I wouldn't have believed a psychiatrist. I felt paralyzed. If I did some-thing, it might be wrong. If I didn't, it might be wrong not to act. I agonized over doubts, deciding the morality of each thought or action. It exhausted me.

I believe the Holy Spirit sent and directed the confessor I happened upon. After two confessions and two meetings, and knowing he was available in between, I experienced ten peaceful years. While I still have questions, I make independent moral decisions without debate.

I'm a manager in a hospital. People respect me at work. I make effective clinical judgments. However, there was a period during which I frequently called the hospital after hours. If I forgot something and something happened to a patient, it would have been my fault. This was the point of neurosis.

I still worry about germs and wash my hands excessively. If I pick up something from the floor, I wash. This inhibits activity. However, I am involved in enough other activities that I cover it well.

Diplomat

A forty-two-year-old diplomat stated:

People view me as successful and a fast riser in my career. Scrupulosity has been a severe detriment to achieving a balanced life. Through counseling by a psychiatric social worker at our parish and reading Scrupulous Anonymous, *I have come to grips with this problem. Although diminished, it is not cured.*

How did it start? This is addressing the essence of scrupulosity. Cause-and-effect relationships elude me. Times of stress — moving, changing jobs, marital problems, highly reflective periods such as Lent — are difficult. Scrupulosity accompanies them. Does scrupulosity or a leaning toward scrupulosity make one flustered in routine situations? Or does scrupulosity feed on itself? I believe faulty religious education instigated my scrupulosity. A focus on sin and its wages rather than on the loving-father concept of God fueled my fears. In its course, scrupulosity has been a curse and a heavy, torturous burden. It has been helpful in sensitizing me to unknown afflictions of others.

Microbiologist

A fifty-nine-year-old professional woman wrote:

No one in my family was scrupulous. Neither were my parents too strict with me. I was a perfectionist about everything, especially morality. At twenty-three, as a novice in a missionary community and looking back over my past, I thought I had committed a serious sin at age sixteen. This caused me suffering. Years later, after talking to a priest, I found that what I thought was sinful was not. My scrupulosity started about this time. I think it occurs when people lack knowledge about what is a sin.

Scrupulosity caused me much suffering and it made me careful about keeping God's law and trying to please Him. After many years I gradually saw it was an illness — the sufferings that united me with Christ. This brought peace. I do not understand why God permits it in us, but I trust

Him. I also understand emotional sufferings of other people because of it.

Right now I am scrupulous in my work as a medical technologist. It is difficult for me to judge how small deviations from the procedure interfere with the accuracy of the test. I must ask another tech.

The Positive Aspects of Scrupulosity

These life stories show that scrupulosity accompanies morality and altruism. A dose of scrupulosity may be good in occupations involving health and safety. When I evaluated public employees, referrals included alcohol and substance abuse problems. The railroad referred one worker for severe OCD. Night security guards had caught him when he broke into the train yard to triple check his work on train brakes. While extreme, this is preferable to no anxiety.

In our survey, we asked respondents to list ways in which scrupulosity was beneficial to their lives. Many persons adamantly insisted it was not. Some wrote in large letters that "IT WAS A CURSE." But the survey showed that many people had found meaning in their suffering. Eleven percent said scrupulosity made them more empathetic, sympathetic, or compassionate. Eighteen percent said that it had made them more moral. Twenty-two percent reported that scrupulosity helped them keep faith in God. Seven percent said that it kept them honest. In a world where we view cleverness or exploitation as achievements, it is comforting to recognize the positive side of scrupulosity.

Chapter 7

MODERATE SCRUPULOSITY: LIVES WITH A CROSS TO BEAR

This chapter focuses on people for whom scrupulosity interferes moderately in their life. They did not identify depression as an intensifying factor. Richness of self-observation graces these accounts, with a high level of introspection and reflection. For many, scrupulosity is combined with growing up in a strict and rigid Catholicism. Nonetheless, it is difficult to conclude to a direct relationship between the two. Many Catholics experienced the same church practices while growing up and did not develop scrupulosity. Survey results provide further understanding of people presented in this chapter. Survey respondents come from relatively intact families. Only 3 percent come from single-parent families. This reflects the mores of the Catholic Church as well as marital trends at the middle of the century. Only 6 percent of respondents in the survey described their family of origin as abusive, and only 6 percent stated there was an alcoholic parent in their family of origin.[31] These figures are lower than those for the general population.

Other statistical information describes family background. Twenty-five percent of respondents reported that scrupulosity had affected their mothers. Twelve percent reported that their father had displayed scrupulous behavior. There was a low incidence of reported scrupulosity among siblings — 4 percent having a scrupulous sister, and 3 percent having a scrupulous brother.

Scrupulous people aren't drawn to each other for marriage. Only 1 percent of respondents reported having a scrupulous spouse. The stories below provide further understanding of moderate Scrup/OCD.

Where Did It Start?

A fifty-four-year-old nurse wrote:

I remember telling a priest that the church caused my scruples. He said, "No, you brought your problems along to the church." He was right, as I now see. Scrupulosity is pretty much under control. I'm in a prayer community which helps me to see that Jesus loves me. I continue to find confession difficult and do not go, since it stirs up embarrassment.

I grew up in a dysfunctional family. My father was probably alcoholic. My mother was unable to communicate love due to a deprived childhood. Both parents were honest and hardworking. When I was about fourteen I went to confession. The old priest picked on me and made me feel worse. He lectured me severely on avoiding scrupulous behavior. He told me not to repeat prayers. After his admonitions, I stopped.

When I was in my early twenties and had five children in five years, I went to a priest in confession. I requested permission to practice rhythm. The priest lectured me. He told me that God would provide and the school would remove the children daily from my care. He said I would create an occasion of sin for my husband. "Men are like boys and they masturbate. Then it will be your fault," the priest said. Years later, another priest superseded this advice and reassured me.

In recent years I have sorted out my relationship with God. God does love me. I used to think he was an ogre, waiting to pounce on me and condemn me. This new view helps me. Confession continues to disturb me. I envy Protestants. They confess directly to God.

This person's account illustrates the difficulties aroused by confession. Many described confession as an ordeal. Despite efforts of helpful confessors, this sacrament causes problems for people with Scrup/OCD. It is interesting that William James viewed the Catholic practice of confession positively:

Within the Christian body, for which repentance of sins has from the beginning been the critical religious act, healthy-mindedness has always come forward with its milder interpretation. Repentance according to such healthy-minded

Christians means *getting away from* the sin, not groaning and writhing over its commission. (James 1982, 128)

Martin Luther, like survey respondents, suffered when he tried to confess:

> When I was a monk, I thought that I was utterly cast away, if at any time I felt the lust of the flesh: that is to say, if I felt any evil motion, fleshly lust, wrath, hatred, or envy against any brother. I assayed many ways to help to quiet my conscience, but it would not be; for the concupiscence and lust of my flesh did always return, so that I could not rest, but was continually vexed with these thoughts: This or that sin thou hast committed: thou art infected with envy, with impatiency, and other sins. (Martyn 1866, 129)

It Started in School

An eighty-six-year-old retired male wrote:

> *My scrupulosity stems from grade school. Nuns and teachers innocently taught us religion from fear rather than love. I still recall our nun explaining eternity. Consider a bird flying around the earth. Every thousand years it touched its beak. When the earth wears down to nothing — eternity begins. Surely one would not want to burn in hell that day! With God being a monster so cruel, who would love such a Being? Of course now I forgive them. They meant well and thought they were doing right.*
>
> *My solution to scrupulosity has been this: "More love and we must accept imperfection."*

Marriage as Cure

While many respondents noted that scrupulosity was detrimental to romance and relationships, one fifty-seven-year-old woman wrote that marriage healed her life:

> *My scrupulosity became clear in my teens. I think an earlier incident in my life provoked it. When I was twenty-two, a wonderful priest helped me be comfortable in receiving Communion. I began go to daily. I still have bouts, but I am*

so much better. I had some very deep fears as I was growing up. For this I spent several years in therapy.

Twenty years ago I married a man who absolutely changed my life. His acceptance of me has created an atmosphere where I believe God has allowed me to live out the talents He has blessed me with.

This respondent believes that scrupulosity "created compassion or at least intensified it in me. I believe it is the ingredient that pushes me toward those in distress."

Cured (90 percent) by Daily Communion

Communion can cause problems for people with Scrup/OCD. For many, a self-induced and torturous confession must precede Communion. Others reported that once they returned to Communion on a regular basis, their scrupulous fears abated.

Overall, 32 percent of respondents reported that they go to Communion on a daily basis. Of the 64 percent who reported going to weekly Mass, only 50 percent reported going to weekly Communion. It appears that reception of this sacrament is difficult for many persons with Scrup/OCD. One respondent, a priest, noted that his scrupulosity took the form of worry that particles of the Host may have scattered during Mass.

Another respondent, a seventy-nine-year-old woman, reported a singular experience that healed her scrupulosity: "A confessor told me not to come back for three months. He told me to go to Communion every time I went to Mass, no matter what I did. This led me to become a daily communicant and cured me at least 90 percent."

While this example may be extreme, it illustrates what behavioral psychologists and St. Ignatius preach: do what you are afraid of. When new habits emerge, anxiety diminishes.

"I have to report potholes"

A sixty-seven-year-old female respondent wrote:

Since I no longer keep a car and so walk a great deal and ride buses, I see things drivers don't see. Large holes in the sidewalk, bent signs, overhanging branches — these are potential dangers. If I can correct the problem, I do. If not, I phone the authorities. It's a good hobby. I try to keep from going to extremes with it but there again, I might not succeed all the time.

This respondent provided some interesting observations concerning her family:

My father was a carpenter, a very good one. Both my parents worked hard and provided a good home for us children. All my life, from birth until about age thirty, I lived with my parents. We resided in a medium-priced but beautiful bungalow my father built. The depression years had begun in my early childhood. Mom had to do laundries at home and housework at other people's homes because it was hard for Dad to find work. Since my mother worked, lack of her presence made me a recluse. I grew up a Lutheran, but decided to leave that faith when I was twelve.

In my twenties Catholicism intrigued me and I enrolled in the Catholic university in our city. With the help of a priest I took instructions as a Catholic, and after that have done well emotionally.

"My scruples returned when my confessor of thirty-six years died"

A retired sixty-five-year-old teacher wrote:

My scrupulosity appeared during freshman year of high school. I was fourteen years old. It was so severe that my mother took me to a psychiatrist. We couldn't afford it for long. I found out I was sane and this was gratifying. I kept repeating prayers and could not go to confession normally. When I finished I would start again. I feared giving consent to sinful urges.

Our family doctor gave me medication, but I don't know what it was. It helped calm my nerves. I was a nervous one. Instead of going to a priest and explaining my problem, I stayed away from confession. This lasted through high school and college. I dated and sang in school concerts and played the piano.

In 1949 I became extremely nervous. Luckily I found a terrific confessor. He assumed control. For thirty-six years I had peace. I felt great. In 1975, my confessor died. Gradually I returned to old nervous ways.

I went to confession not often, but regularly. The past sins bothered me so I began to confess them and made a general confession in 1977. Still not completely at peace, I kept telling various past sins and thought I had to tell every number for each sin I confessed. Everything was serious sin.

My current confessor understands me and helps me but not in the same way as the one I had for thirty-six years.

"I can't distinguish between a fantasy and an intention"

Many respondents are plagued by "bad thoughts." They fear that they take pleasure in them or intend to carry them out. Therapy provides people with Scrup/OCD the freedom to discuss these thoughts.[32] As noted in chapter 13, there are passages in the current *Catechism of the Catholic Church* which may cause undue anxiety in scrupulous people. Research into behavior therapy suggests behavioral therapies are more effective with behaviors than thoughts.[33] But since mental manifestations of Scrup/OCD may be harder to cure than rituals, perhaps empathic therapists and confessors may provide healing encouragement in this area.

A forty-four-year-old married teacher reported the following: "Many times my thoughts have no reason. When I have obsessive sexual thoughts, I wonder if this is a sin. I have such a hard time distinguishing between a fantasy and an intention."

A positive aspect of scrupulosity reported by this woman was that it made her seek professional help. "I am learning and changing," she said. She reported that therapy had helped greatly.

"God saves us"

Readers will recall our discussion concerning Martin Luther. He treated his scrupulosity by believing that God's grace, not our efforts, saves us. A fifty-six-year-old married respondent reported coming to a similar conclusion. However, even with good adjustment, scruples still persist for him:

> *I feel I must go to confession before Communion. I am conscious of what I see on television or hear on the radio. If I see or hear something questionable, or a bad joke, I keep a straight face. I watch carefully what I see on the street and do daily battle to control impure ideas and thoughts.*
>
> *I grew up in an Irish immigrant home. Both parents attended Mass. There was some tension in my house and we invited few guests. I was a shy schoolboy, with little or no participation in sports. My mother worried about sin and she even asked me questions about various things. My mother depended on me too much. This made me worry even more.*
>
> *I married my wife seventeen years ago and we have no children. I was about a week short of my fortieth birthday when I got married. Fatherhood scared me.*
>
> *Scrupulosity has prevented me from neglecting my religion and moral obligations. It makes me do my daily work and use time wisely. Because of scrupulosity I avoid conflict with fellow workers. In my prayer life, a spirit of humility exists. Scrupulosity keeps me aware of God, with a duty and debt to my fellow man. We don't save ourselves — God does. Still, I wonder how the seeds of scrupulosity were sown in a twelve-year-old schoolboy.*
>
> *The advice in* Scrupulous Anonymous, *that we do not save ourselves — God saves us — helps me. Some priests who hear my confessions are comforting. They encourage me to finish. They ask, "Is there anything else that is disturbing you?" This leaves a deep imprint and puts me at ease. Does it stop the scrupulous impulse? No, but it is kindness I always remember. Similar words were spoken to me in a Redemptorist church in Ireland, and I have not forgotten them. Perhaps I will be scrupulous forever. For me it would be a nightmare if we did not have dedicated souls hearing our confessions.*

"Can I help my daughters head it off?"

A forty-two-year-old male fitness specialist wrote:

> Puberty intensified my scrupulosity during the sixth and seventh grades. I remember the anguish of going to confession to relate my impure thoughts and preoccupation with looking at the female anatomy. I thought every temptation was a sin. Confession relieved me and afterward I felt at peace with God. Then the cycle repeated.
>
> In high school I confessed "prolonged kissing." I can't remember how long "prolonged" was. Today I don't worry about the time element.
>
> When I went to college my scruples flew out the window. I started drinking. Not a real boozer, I drank almost every Friday night with the boys...I became more involved sexually with my fiancée. We stopped short of intercourse as we worried about having a child out of marriage.
>
> We remained married for ten years. After my divorce I joined a small charismatic Bible church. I learned about Scriptures. I remember one electrifying realization. During one Bible study, the pastor reminded us that Jesus had taken the burden and guilt of our sin upon himself. I thought — you know, "I've been trying to shoulder it for years! So that's what I've missed as a Catholic!"
>
> I've been dating and have had several serious relationships. I wonder if I will ever get married again. I keep looking for Miss Right. What I really want to strive to do is be the right person, not find the right person. The prospect of another failed marriage frightens me.
>
> Today I'm back in the Catholic Church and participating in the charismatic renewal. I'm learning to trust God and to do it day by day. I'm reaching out to new friends. I'm trying to find the right balance in my life. I have two daughters and we relate well. I wonder, "Can I help my daughters head off scrupulosity?"

"In any moment, I could commit a serious sin"

A twenty-four-year-old unmarried female computer programmer wrote:

Mostly I worry about committing sins about impurity. Sometimes it is hard for me to walk, sit, or stand normally. These provoke feelings of impurity. People at work tease me in a friendly way about being bow-legged, which I am not.

I walk that way because of fears. I try to walk normally in front of people, but sometimes forget. It is also hard to sit normally. Much of the time at work I sit on the edge of my chair because I think I might give in to bad feelings. I never lie on my stomach anymore when I sleep, and rarely on my side for the same reasons mentioned above. I sleep in a certain position most of the time and don't usually move.

I blaspheme and think impure thoughts. These trouble me. When they come, I shake my head to try to get rid of them. I try not to do this in public but sometimes I slip and so I pretend it is just a bad habit.

What worries me is that at any moment and in only a few seconds I could commit a serious sin. The only remedy is confession. I worry about what I've done until I confess it; then it's over. The problem is that I fall or worry again and need to go back.

This respondent's description of inner battles suggests how scrupulosity can be especially horrifying. The specter of eternal damnation multiplies anxieties.

"Scruples affect my sister, too; her hands are always red and raw"

I have spoken of the close relationship between scrupulosity and obsessive compulsive disorder. This next case suggests why it is important for helpers to look for OCD in addition to scrupulosity. A fifty-four-year-old married man in a professional position noted:

My scrupulosity is fear of going to confession and confessing correctly. I haven't been to confession for two years now. Although now I have very few symptoms of scrupulosity, I fear that going back to confession will bring some of them back.

My scruples started at age sixteen. In my first work experience I became involved with people who told "off color" stories. At first I did not confess these. I rationalized them away. When guilt feeling got so strong I confessed them as well as all previous confessions. For many years I kept going to confession every two weeks. I rarely went to Communion more than once after each confession. It was so hard for me to keep a clear conscience. When I got married at age thirty, I stopped going to confession so much. I moved and couldn't go off to churches where I was unknown. After having a good confessor and then spiritual direction for several years, I now go to Communion weekly.

In my birth family, scrupulosity afflicts my older sister. She is immaculate; her hands are always red and raw.

They Keep Up with Their Lives

Despite internal suffering and conflict, many scrupulous persons meet the primary demands of their lives. Thirty-four percent of respondents noted that when their scrupulosity was at its worst, it affected friendships very little. Percentages of those reporting very little effect on romance, marriage, school, and work were respectively 22 percent, 23 percent, 34 percent, and 24 percent. Only 15 percent of respondents noted that scrupulosity interfered with having children. This finding differs from reports in the OCD literature. Many persons with OCD express concern over whether or not their symptoms will affect their ability to be a parent. The Catholic orientation of this group of persons may account for the willingness to have children.

The next chapter looks at persons who suffer from problems of even greater complexity. For these people Scrup/OCD and other potent emotional problems coexist.

Chapter 8

DEPRESSION AND SCRUPULOSITY

In our survey many readers reported that they also suffered from depression. In the professional literature on obsessive compulsive disorder, research suggests that depression often accompanies OCD. Is it the depression that leads to OCD? Or do the crippling and time-consuming rituals produce such a loss of control and isolation from people and rewarding activities that it leads to depression? These same questions are relevant to Scrup/OCD. All respondents cited in this chapter acknowledged depression as part of their experience in grappling with Scrup/OCD. Many effective treatments exist for depression. Some new strategies using cognitive behavior therapy are particularly effective.

The traditional Freudian view cited "anger turned inward" as the cause of depression. The cure was to locate the source of the anger and deal with it in therapy, which often took years. Critics of this approach have pointed out that patients could become more depressed as they felt even more helpless about their lives. Many persons with Scrup/OCD have a tendency to "spin their wheels" in such therapy. They are adept at reviewing past actions.

Cognitive behavior therapists believe depression results from a lack of control. Rewarding relationships slip away. Boredom increases. Despair and despondency result. Cognitive therapists favor action. They help people set goals, teach them how to turn negative thoughts into positive ones, and stress appropriate emotions.[34]

Current medications approved for treating obsessive compulsive disorder all began as antidepressants. Researchers discovered that each has additional anti-OCD benefits. Thus appropriate medication provides both an anti-OCD and antidepressant effect.

The stories below describe the combination of depression and

Scrup/OCD. As we shall see, people who are depressed don't experience the joyful and hopeful elements of their religious tradition.

"I don't receive Holy Communion anymore"

A sixty-year-old man on disability wrote:

> *To achieve peace of mind, I stopped receiving Holy Communion. I don't go to confession. I feel more at ease. I've been going to daily Mass for twenty-eight years. I've stopped Communion the last three and a half years. I feel more comfortable now.*
>
> *My father was a hardworking steelworker and my mother was a devoted housewife. My grandmother lived with us and helped to bring us up. Both my mother and grandmother were very religious. I never got along with my brother. Even now we live in the same house, and we still ignore each other. He is reclusive and keeps to himself with the door shut. I accepted every word from the priests and nuns. In my eyes they were perfect.*
>
> *I became aware of my scrupulosity when I was sixteen. I struggled with confession and receiving Communion every first Friday. I went to a Catholic school and we went as a group. When I was eighteen I stopped confession because of torment about past sins. I saw my first psychiatrist at age nineteen. A priest advised me to stop. At that time Catholicism and psychiatry didn't mix. I went into the Army, fell into serious sin, and saw a Catholic psychiatrist three times weekly for a year. He was the couch type with an M.D. I dropped him when he referred me back to a priest.*
>
> *Back home again, I worked until I had a nervous breakdown. I sought out a priest who heard my general confession. Then I began seeing a psychiatrist, which continued for twenty-eight years. He prescribed mind-altering drugs such as Parnate, Stelazine, and Valium. I was able to go to confession and Communion without any trouble from the past. The present didn't bother me either. I stayed in the state of grace. Then the past started to come alive. For the next twelve years confession became hell, every three months.*

Somehow I struggled and managed to get to Communion every day. Finally, I stopped going to Holy Communion. I still go to daily Mass. I have not bothered my confessor and I don't have the same desire to confess. I leave it all up to God.

Once a priest asked me in confession, "What did you do?" Since then I must tell every detail. It's like drawing a complex picture. I envy people who make simple confessions.

"I'm not as scrupulous since Vatican II"

A fifty-eight-year-old widow stated:

I never felt I was a severe case of scrupulosity. I'm not as scrupulous as I was before Vatican II. I'm more peaceful. I don't see sin in common, everyday events.

I was a "change of life" child and had one sister who was twenty years old when I was born. She was good and generous to me. Our home, though, was not peaceful. I went to high school and then night school.

Vatican II changed some of my scruples as did my marriage to a wonderful man. I wish I had received this broad overview of life in general earlier. I would have been more peaceful, contented, and happy.

I think scrupulosity made me compassionate toward others who are less fortunate — the sick, dying, lonely, and others I meet. I'm extremely sensitive and emotional and take life too seriously. I should lighten up, and I wish I could have accomplished this with my husband. I miss him very deeply. I hate being a widow. This is the worst pain I have ever endured.

"In my desperation I looked for answers, mostly in books"

A seventy-one-year-old homemaker and widow wrote:

My scruples mostly concern fear of hurting other people and also duties that I feel may be essential but are very difficult and often embarrassing to perform.

All my life I have been extremely scrupulous, as far back as I can remember. In my early teens my mother recognized the symptoms and sent me to see a priest. He was kind but not helpful. Sometimes I just had to stop receiving the sacraments in order to get relief. I think that I was scrupulous about anything and everything. I had a fear of germs and contamination and still do, especially with the appearance of AIDS, Herpes, and other new diseases.

I finally tried a psychiatrist but that didn't help much. The drugs helped some. I don't remember their names; it was years ago. After a while I had side effects and stopped taking them. I haven't taken them in years.

In the past ten years I have made much progress through Scrupulous Anonymous. It saved my life. It took some doing but I was finally able to apply the "Let go and let God" slogan to my life. This really helped. I think I will never be fully healed. I still have difficulty with germs and contamination. My scruples have been worse at times. They would always get worse when I had problems or sadness in my life.

In my desperation, I looked for answers, mostly in books. I learned much from all this reading. It helped me to focus on what is important.

"It helped me have a set of values"

A retired dean at a college wrote:

I make it a point not to offend God. I highly value honesty and integrity: to do everything perfectly — but this is not possible and that causes me stress. I want to meet goals and to do so immediately. When I don't, I get upset. I judge people too hastily on their moral values.

In my birth family, we met our debts of going to church and practicing our faith openly. I am the father of six children and strive to give examples of church-going on a daily basis. I inherited chronic depression. My treatment involves antidepressants, which help significantly.

Scrupulosity helped me have values and pass them on to my children. I am putting my life in God's hands. I really do love God!

"I was dating a married gangster; he told me I wasn't going to heaven because I was doing bad things"

A forty-five-year-old married female wrote:

I'm always worrying about my relationship with God. Sometimes I trust him, sometimes not. Does he get angry when I don't? Trust is hard. A relative molested me when I was a child. My first husband beat me for twenty-two years. I broke every commandment. I remarried. I worry if the church approved my marriage. Some Christians say annulments don't count. Catholics say they do. What does God say? This confuses me. I cannot receive the sacraments. I'm always wrong. The Church forgives other sins, even adultery or murder. If you dare remarry, the church blacklists you. She denies the sacraments and Communion. You're always outside, looking in.

I now go to Mass every few days. I listen to Christian radio and watch Christian TV and read books. Going to therapy made my scrupulosity worse.

In the past I had been dating a married gangster. He told me I wasn't going to heaven because I did bad things. When he said that, I knew he was right. My scrupulosity from childhood returned. God must have felt my sorrow and called me back to him. Realizing my sinfulness helped me cry out to God. Someone murdered my gangster friend. The killer eludes police. God used him to reach me in the sorry state I was in.

"The psychologist suggested I go to bed with some gal and that would cure my problems"

A forty-eight-year-old male professional wrote:

I have been scrupulous since my teens. I feared my father. I expected punishment that bordered on violence. A sister and brother got slugged a few times. My approach was to do what my father asked because I feared him. My mother accepted verbal abuse and other shortcomings, to do God's will.

Scrupulosity was a constant mental shadow which questioned everything I did for fear of committing a mortal

*sin. The rejection that I received at home and in the com-
munity was reinforced at Church. I confessed my sexual
sins to a priest. My self-esteem plummeted. After about ten
years I overcame the sinful habit, but scrupulous obsession
remained. I am not sure if my sins were really grave ones.*

*When I was sixteen the fear of committing a sexual sin
obsessed me. To prevent any wet dreams, I tied myself in bed
so that I could not turn. I even lost the circulation in my feet.
I obsessed over repeating penance. I would say it without
interruption to the point where I thought I was crazy.*

*I saw a psychologist in college. The psychologist suggested
I go to bed with some gal and that would cure my problems.
I did not trust or respect him after that.*

*I have suffered other problems. A fear of God has kept
me on the straight and narrow path. My marriage is happy,
but I still have my problem of scrupulosity.*

"My scrupulosity flares up at income tax time"

A forty-five-year-old female receptionist wrote:

*I don't receive Communion often or at all. When I avoid the
sacraments, my scrupulosity lessens. My scrupulosity ebbs
and flows. It gets worse around income tax time, with all the
official forms to file and sign. I married, in the church, a divorced man. This also flares up and bothers me — is he truly
morally "free" of that past marriage? Did we make clear
all the circumstances of his first marriage when we spoke to
the priest? Does the church truly not recognize his first marriage? I feel guilty about meeting him when he was not yet
separated. His three children feel that he abandoned them. It
goes on and on.*

*Although I am not 100 percent sure, I feel my scrupu-
losity began in the third grade. Innocently, my cousin and I
used to go into the church and light votive candles. We were
unaware it was a sin. We just liked to light them. A nun discovered us one day in the act and heavily impressed upon
us our badness. She said we committed a wrong act and it
scared us. I was always a timid, "eager-to-please" child with
many fears.*

When I met my husband, I forgot about scrupulosity and never received Communion again until we were married. This was only after going to confession to list our premarital sins. He is not scrupulous and my scrupulosity surpasses his understanding. He was Lutheran and he doesn't realize how troubled I am by all of this.

May God help all us scrupulous persons in this life. I hope he'll welcome our tear-stained faces into his heavenly light, when he'll wash away our guilt with his love.

"My scruples started fifty years ago"

A seventy-year-old widow wrote:

My scruples started fifty years ago, when we lost our healthy five-year-old little boy quite suddenly. This devastated me. It shattered and changed my life. I wanted to see my little boy again, and the only way to do this was to get to heaven. That meant I must not have any sins. That was the beginning. Sometimes I felt better, sometimes not so good, and in between a living hell. I was full of sin.

I didn't know I was scrupulous at the time. In fact, I didn't even know about scruples at all. I just thought I was a bad sinner. That's not to say I didn't sin. One day I went to see a priest because I had to cure myself, once and for all. He told me I was scrupulous. That's when I found out. It's been a hard struggle ever since, but I never gave up praying and asking God for help. Sometimes it seems hopeless. I am much better now, nothing compared to what I was, but I still panic at times.

Scrupulosity helped me get closer to God. I had become careless about my religion and I guess God wanted me back, but it's been a very hard struggle. I hope when God calls me, He will have mercy on me and forgive all my sins.

"It has saddened my entire life"

An eighty-year-old woman wrote that she keeps busy "grocery shopping, working around my house and yard, and managing rental property." She reflected on a lifetime of scrupulosity:

I will begin by telling you what I think caused my scruples. When I was about fifteen or sixteen years old, the sister at school said that every sin against the sixth and ninth commandments was mortal. To someone who never wanted to commit a mortal sin, that was very frightening.

When I was seventeen, I was going daily to Mass and Communion. One morning I had a hat on with a wide brim on it. The priest spoke to me as he went to give me Communion and told me to put my head back, which of course was unnecessary. Just the idea of the priest having to speak to me, at such a sacred time, shocked me. I have never since that day been able to receive Communion in peace.

For the next thirteen years I managed to go to confession and Communion once a year to fulfill my Easter duty. By this time my scruples had become so bad, I didn't go to Communion or confession for thirty-nine years. During all these years I was in constant anxiety, always praying and asking God to give me the mental ability to make a good confession.

This person went through her entire life, suffering silently. Priests did not help her; she didn't seek out a therapist.

Eleven years ago I got sick and asked for a priest and made a general confession. After examining my conscience for about an hour, I immediately became anxious, feeling I had not taken enough time. I wished I had listed other sins.

So this is how I am today. I worry day and night, and at times I have to lay it aside so I won't become ill. I am always asking God to help me make a good confession and begging him to cure me of this condition.

"Peace of mind is what I yearn for"

A forty-five-year-old female social worker, in a position of responsibility, wrote:

I have preoccupations with sins committed even after I have confessed. Mistakes are extremely difficult for me. I feel bad even when I can't avoid them. I have been in therapy for nearly ten years. It has helped, as has spiritual direction.

I grew up as the oldest of eight children, with other extended family members living in the home. My father suffered from alcohol addiction. My mother experienced bulimia. I had major responsibilities from a very young age and was physically and sexually abused.

As a teenager, having sex with a boyfriend led to extreme distress and a period of confusion. Getting married at age fifteen was not a solution. For an extended period after we broke up, I tried to isolate myself. I was very lonely after high school and would find myself in sexual relationships again and again. Eventually, I resolved this with marriage.

After six years of marriage, I had an affair and became extremely despondent. This was the only way I believed I could get out of the marriage. The immaturity on both our parts was debilitating. I suffered during this period. It was the closest I ever came to a nervous breakdown.

After I became divorced, I lost the desire for casual sex, but I was unable to stop. I got an abortion. This took me to the depth of depression. My eating went out of control. This past year I have become seriously involved in a Twelve Step program of recovery for an eating disorder. I try to attend a meeting every day.

I yearn for peace of mind. Trying to learn new behaviors and learning new ideas helps me have hope. Being a born-again Catholic helps me with my faith walk with Jesus.

"I wish I had been born Protestant"

A sixty-two-year-old married female housewife wrote:

I used to be scrupulous about impure thoughts. I thought I overcame this, but now I'm overscrupulous about everything else. I'm a fanatic, I guess. I've turned into a perfectionist. I think everything I do is a mortal sin no matter how hard I try not to do it.

My birth family was quite church-oriented. My father was deeply religious. My one brother became a priest. We four children had a Catholic school education. We practice religion differently. My husband attends Sunday Mass; that's all. He says his religion is in his heart.

As a child, people called me a trouble-maker. Sometimes my parents called me "beloved brat." They did not mean it affectionately. As an adult, I feel that my family treated me as a second-class citizen. My brother, the priest, confirmed it when he referred to me once as "the least stone."

I would say that confession as a teenager made me worse. My scruples began when I was about thirteen or fourteen. Confession became a terrible ordeal. To make it worse, the nuns marched us to school on the Thursday before the First Friday. They forced us to go to confession. Only when I was a senior in high school did my pastor stop this practice. Now, confession is still an ordeal. Some priests do not help at all. Confession has been the bane of my existence. I wish I had been born Methodist. If I didn't have a brother who was a priest, I might have turned Protestant.

"Sorry, Lord, it's just me"

My scrupulosity is gone but some remembrances frighten me until I regain my spiritual balance. Sometimes when I'm tired I get scrupulous. I tell myself chemicals cause it. This helps me believe God will not demean me. Then I say, "Sorry, Lord, it's just me." After that, no matter how horrible the thought or temptation, or the remembrance of past horrors, I dismiss it from my mind, with full knowledge that — perhaps after a good night's sleep, or even within the hour — the Lord will make me find some humor in my humbling situation. Time heals the wounds.

Before I was a school-age child, my parents sent me to live with relatives for three years. They taught me the Catholic faith. I went to Catholic schools. I remember trying to convert my parents.

At their worst, my scruples were incapacitating. At one point I actually had no friends. I became untouchable and did not date. Jesus healed me and this kept the problem from getting worse. Then I married a person I love and could be comfortable with. In lighter moments, I think we display similar neuroses.

Throughout my life I have tried to treat my scrupulosity in various ways. I have never seen a therapist or talked to my doctor. Prayer and the rosary did not always help. I would go to confession but wouldn't talk about what was troubling me.

When I was young I thought I was crazy, so I had to keep the crazy part to myself. The result was that the "crazies" grew and festered until I began to think that suicide was a possible answer. I lacked courage for it, though. I thought I needed a psychiatrist, but I thought it would be too expensive.

I eventually developed phobias about urinating, and could not go to a bathroom in public places. This led to a severely disturbed social life. At work I would restrict fluid intake. I could go to the bathroom only if no one was in the lady's room. I couldn't bear to have anyone hear the sound of urine splashing, thinking it was mine. I envied anyone who could urinate within the hearing of another.

Scrupulosity has kept me safe. I withdrew from life and exposed myself to fewer problems. As my faith went from childish to childlike, I gained a marvelous appreciation for God. When he healed me, gradually my relationship deepened. I continue to have feelings of love and gratitude.

During my first seven or eight years of marriage, I failed my husband, myself, my children, and even the cat. Yet, I have had faith, hope, and trust. Bedrock faith in God keeps me going.

"It is worse than physical pain"

A sixty-eight-year-old woman wrote:

Study on scrupulosity is long overdue. Catholic newspapers or magazines don't mention it. Priests ignore it in sermons. I'm afraid we don't know to help it and cure it.

I've suffered with scrupulosity for about thirty years now. I'm now about 98 percent cured, and have been for about ten years. It was traumatic, and at times excruciating, and made me miserable. It is worse than physical pain, I believe, and I have had surgery three times.

The family I grew up in was as follows. My father was very rigid and he beat my mother. My mother was kind, compassionate, and loving — but she was not affectionate. There was no affection from my father. My sisters and I are close. One of them had scruples.

Prayer helped me. Before about two and one half years of psychiatric counseling for obsessive compulsive neurosis I had what I'd call a breakdown. I couldn't function normally. I could not get my work here at home done. I'd go to bed at two or four in the morning. I washed my hands, arms, and legs. I feared germs or chemicals in the soap. The thought of fire terrified me. The psychiatrist never dealt with or mentioned the religious scruples, even though he was a Catholic. He hospitalized me for thirty days and he gave me shock treatments. I feel family support, mostly from my husband, helped me the most. Perhaps the therapy and the medicine helped. I had group therapy. I followed this by attending Recovery meetings for about nine months. They did not help.

There may have been an underlying fear of dying and going to hell. I had a rigid priest for catechism class. I was a tender, emotional child and adult.

"The Catholic Girl's Guide *made me more scrupulous*"

A forty-two-year-old woman who works as a writer and editor wrote:

I worry about whether I have seriously sinned. I fear I've hurt someone's reputation by talking about their faults. I worry about sins I forgot to confess.

I grew up in a fairly happy family. My mother had tantrums when we three kids got on her nerves too much. These may have made me prone to scrupulosity. There was a minimum of sibling rivalry. My father was an alcoholic at times. But he treated us well. He was quite an intellectual and opened my mind. I went to Catholic schools for twelve years. One teacher had tantrums like my mother.

When I was an adolescent, I read a book called The Catholic Girl's Guide. *This dated from the early 1900s. I viewed it strictly and this made me more scrupulous.*

My mother supported me when I finally told her my problem. My scrupulosity flared up when a priest preached a parish mission. I went overboard trying to be good afterward. It also flared up as I was becoming engaged. It drove me nuts trying to figure out the definition of sinful passionate kissing. After I divorced and was single again, I found it hard to relax with some men at first when dating. I was very careful not to go too far. These fears gradually dissipated with my confessor's help.

I am a workaholic and perfectionist. Not to the degree that it hurts relationships. It requires discipline for me to stop working when so much remains undone.

Scrupulosity has made some other trials appear less traumatic. It has drawn me to a terrific spiritual director and a prayer group I might have otherwise not heard of. My ability to focus on detail has won me accolades and awards at work.

I'd like to find out more about what bothers other scrupulous people and what caused their troubles.

"To have perfection in everything I do"

A fifty-seven-year-old female homemaker wrote:

Scruples in my life take the form of obsessive compulsive behavior. I dwell on the letter of the law more than the spirit. I'm a perfectionist in everything I do.

In my estimation my home environment was stressful. My father passed away when I was an infant. My mother was a very demanding woman. At age four my mother remarried. My stepfather was a pessimist. I have difficulty trying to describe my home life. It was a mixture of happiness and sadness.

Severe scruples became part of my life at age sixteen. Until the age of twenty-nine, I handled them on my own. Two special confessors helped me. My marriage, as well as the births of two of my children, made my scruples more intense. At these times, I saw a therapist. The Scrupulous Anonymous newsletter has helped me.

The normal level of scruples returned until I had major surgery. Then I was in a deep depression. Dr. Conrad Baars of San Antonio, Texas, treated me. I consider him to be one of the finest doctors I have ever met. He has died, but he lives on through his writings, which help me greatly.

"The doctors checked me for a brain tumor, but there was no sign"

A fifty-four-year-old female, a married teacher, wrote:

I handle my scrupulosity with the help of books. I still have a problem fretting about mosquitos. I worry if electrical appliances are turned off.

When I married my husband, scruples hit hard, and I didn't know why or what it was. I was depressed and had severe headaches, muscle aches, and body tightness. The doctors checked for a brain tumor, but there was no sign. A doctor prescribed Valium, and this helped temporarily.

If my parents loved me more, I may not have had this affliction. I pretended to act like a clown in the classroom. No one figured out that I was lonely and depressed.

My husband's love and concern helped me to recover. He loved me for myself. This convinced me that I am lovable. I can see how important it is to instill the love concept into everyone. I love kids, and I enjoy them. They made me feel good when I worked for them, and my self-esteem improved. I still have contact with friends I've made over the years in various places where I've taught. I love them, and they love me in return.

My birth family has no idea of what I've suffered or endured. They just figured I have a nervous problem and stress in teaching. My mom and sister have had some flareups, too. Everyone in my family has nervous surges. We have a close relationship in spite of the past. One learns to forgive and forget and make the most of life.

I seldom have a headache now, and only take a vitamin pill and calcium pills. My health is good. I have a sense of peace now, and I enjoy life.

"I'm afraid to travel far from home because I seldom feel in a state of grace"

A forty-four-year-old female homemaker wrote:

I'm afraid to travel far from home because I seldom feel in the state of grace. On Saturdays I am nervous and feel I should go to confession. If I don't, I make myself sick.

I grew up in a family with two loving parents. To the best of my knowledge, my brothers and sisters escaped scrupulosity.

I visit the church before trips, praying for safe trips. My scrupulosity gets worse when it's time to go to confession. I keep going over everything in my mind. I sound like a worse person than I am because I can't leave anything out. Forgiveness eludes me because I forget to tell sins. I try to say everything so I am covered.

My scrupulosity flares up around holidays when people go to confession. The somber thinking of Advent and Lent encourages my scrupulosity. It lessens in spring and summer because these seasons are more carefree, except when it's time to go to confession. Now I trust God to get me through.

I am not a wild person at all. If scrupulosity has helped me at all, it has kept me from doing spontaneous things that are wrong.

"It's a combination of genetics, family, and Catholic upbringing"

A thirty-six-year-old teacher wrote:

My scrupulous behavior is better than in my teens or twenties. It caused me great unhappiness and distress. Through therapy, prayer, Scrupulous Anonymous, and other sources, I have achieved relief. This is not a cure. I still obsess and worry. My hypoglycemia magnifies my obsessive spells.

My family included six brothers and sisters and my parents. My mother was an emotionally unstable and rather obsessive person. Although my father worked hard, he withdrew and did not talk to us. Some of my brothers and sisters have had emotional problems. There was no sense of secu-

rity or unconditional love in my household. It was a place of anxiety and mistrust.

I can't say for certain what caused my scrupulosity. I believe it was a combination of rigid religious training in Catholic school, a dysfunctional home environment, and my own genetic make-up. I felt I had to be perfect and could not make mistakes in any area of my life. So my scrupulosity and my obsession went beyond religious matters. I also felt extremely responsible for everything and everyone, perhaps because my mother made me feel responsible for her problems and unhappiness. And being in control was very important to me — because security and control were often absent in my childhood home.

Scrupulosity kept me from taking drugs when many of my friends were. It helped me by leading me toward a better understanding of God. I feel very fortunate that I have been able to overcome scrupulosity and obsessive behavior to some extent in my life.

"Did Jesus ever find scrupulous people, and how did he treat them?"

A forty-seven-year-old housewife from Ireland wrote:

I have been scrupulous since childhood. Suddenly, there was this fear of hell. The schools talked about children who died and went to hell, and my grandmother gave me a prayer book that said there were many gates to hell. When I was eleven, I started repeating confessions to make sure they were perfect. If a priest was sympathetic, I thought he did not understand me. I suspected this warning was coming true: "a blind one cannot guide another blind one or they will fall into the pit." I did not know that I had a treatable disease. I confessed to different priests who did not know anything about me. It got worse. I only went to Communion after confession and it had to be on the same day, in case I committed sins. There was a great worry about sacrilege.

From age eighteen on, confusion reigned. One priest told me that it was a mortal sin to kiss boyfriends on the lips. Boyfriends rejected me. By the time I was twenty-eight I

*thought I could not go on like this and I felt miserable. I
felt depressed after a boyfriend whom I loved very much left
me. I had a depression and the scrupulosity became awful.
It was the first of many terrible crises.*

*I saw psychiatrists but they did not understand my prob-
lem. One said I should embrace and kiss boyfriends. I did
that but felt terrible because I did not love this particular one.*

*I fell in love with a man who loved me in return. I
thought this would make me better. It was a big mistake.
Marriage multiplied my problems and I had a terrible crisis
of scrupulosity.*

*Therapy with psychiatrists was advised by a priest, but
here they do not have time to listen as they prefer to give you
tranquilizers. Besides, in a country where most psychiatrists
are not Roman Catholics, how can they understand?*

*Now I go to a confessor who understands my problems
and I have become a little better. At least I can function
in life. I have a son and I pray for him to have a right
conscience, not one that is lax or scrupulous. But I have difficulty in making decisions and still have to keep consulting
my confessor. I talk to him and ask questions on occasions,
but I still feel very mixed up.*

From Depression to Hopefulness

As awareness of treatment approaches is made available to sufferers of Scrup/OCD, I think a sense of collective hopefulness
will begin to emerge among people who share this condition.
As psychotherapists and physicians become more aware of the
specialized needs of those who grapple with Scrup/OCD, their
treatments will become more effective and their healing will be
much greater. One of the great Christian virtues is hope, and a
spirit of optimism and courage (see also chapter 15) seems fitting
among people with Scrup/OCD and their helpers.

Chapter 9

OTHER PROBLEMS INTENSIFY SCRUPULOSITY

Scrupulosity can occur in combination with other emotional problems. This can make understanding and helping the person more difficult. Persons with Scrup/OCD can suffer from bipolar disorder, anxiety disorders, eating disorders, and thought disorders. They display alcohol and substance abuse problems. The complexity of problems can be staggering. Each problem area may need direct focus. The interaction of several conditions may make the determination of the correct medication very difficult.

In recent years mental health professionals have become more sensitive to treating persons suffering from separate psychological problems. Psychologists use words like "dual diagnosis" or "comorbidity" to describe these cases.

Some persons may not seek treatment. They fear therapists will reduce religious feelings to other concerns or ignore them. This is sad when people have Scrup/OCD with another problem, and it robs them of effective treatment.

Eloquence, intelligence, and deep pain were expressed by respondents who suffered from scrupulosity combined with other maladies. They wrote movingly of treatment that didn't help. Others wrote of finally getting a mental health professional who was able to help. Some wrote that a combined approach — a mental health professional working alongside a priest, for example — was the best.

This chapter may be of special interest to clergy as well as professional therapists. A nonprofessional counselor should not take on a case that is too complex. For example, it is not in the interest of clients for pastoral counselors to treat them for problems such as manic depression, anorexia, or schizophrenia. Harm can be done. While we realize that labels can harm, it is also true that a reasoned mental health diagnosis, made by a mental health professional, can open avenues of treatment and hope. It is important for pastoral counselors to refer difficult situations to competent professional therapists.

There are pitfalls for professional therapists also. They may acknowledge or treat only the panic disorder or the eating disorder. If Scrup/OCD remains untreated, therapy suffers. Persons with Scrup/OCD may not comply with helpers who rebuff their religious experiences.

Following is a discussion of conditions mentioned in the survey together with Scrup/OCD.

Scrupulosity and Bipolar Disorder

Manic depression, or bipolar disorder, as DSM IV calls it, can be crippling. It robs the sufferer of family and employment. In manic phases, sufferers may display bizarre behaviors, run up large credit card bills, travel to different states, act promiscuously, or destroy property. When depressed, they may appear lifeless, stay in bed all day, not eat, and even be suicidal. Persons with these behaviors may need hospital evaluation and treatment.

Psychiatrists have treated bipolar disorder effectively since the early 1950s. Evaluation and treatment by a physician is crucial. Psychiatrists report that with proper medication 75 percent to 85 percent of people with bipolar disorder can be helped.

A forty-five-year-old divorced man reported that he had taken Tegretol to control manic depression. For seven years his condition had remitted. He wrote eloquently about bipolar disorder and Scrup/OCD combined. Hopefulness was his signature: "As cured as I've ever been." He wrote:

My problems with scrupulosity began in the seventh and eighth grades. As I look back, these factors come to mind. My mother and father were perfect in my mind. A nun who I think was having problems with scrupulosity herself was passing a fear of God on to us. There was a fire and brimstone sermon. I feared confession. There wasn't much counseling in confession to help me understand my sins. I was just confessing my fear and my confessor's lack of counseling worked against me.

Through my teen years a "Dr. Jekyll and Mr. Hyde" life started. Confession worked for a day or two. Then I had a sin of a bad thought. Then I gave up and felt I was going to hell. I went back and forth like this until I was twenty-one and got married.

I thought I would solve this problem with sex. I fought with bad thoughts about lusting after women. I felt if I didn't turn the other way just driving through town, I was desiring others. Confession did help me somewhat at this point in my life.

When I was around thirty years old I became involved with a charismatic prayer group and felt free from old rules. I felt God's saving power. God forgave all my sins now and forever.

My mind could not take all this new and wild speaking in tongues, prophecy, and miracles. I got too high and ended up on a mental ward. I was high and then low over this period. Through this period I lost my job and sold my house and farm. My wife left me. After my divorce, my scrupulosity was at its highest. With treatment and work I stayed healthy. These helped me: the SA newsletter, books I have read, counseling with priests and nuns, my psychiatrist, friends, a loving God, and leaving the real sin in my life up to God.

I see parallels between my manic depression and my scrupulosity. First, when I feel high, there is a feeling related to scrupulosity of being "the perfect person" and doing everything right. In terms of manic depression, I feel so high to God then that I could talk to him, and he talks back.

At my low points, scrupulosity gives guilt, a sense of sins, and cross-examining myself as a person. I feel no good as a person. The corresponding depression involves having no interest in living and feeling like a worthless person.

Another person, a forty-six-year-old married housewife who had struggled with manic depression and scrupulosity for many years, wrote: "God calls lowly, stupid, incapable people to make them what he wants them to be. The rest of humanity is born with a full deck of cards."

This woman provided an eloquent description of growing up with family problems, scrupulosity, and manic depression. She had been hospitalized and used confession, therapy, spiritual direction, and reading books to make herself feel better. She reported that medication made her condition worse. She wrote:

> *When I was little I heard a song "Bad, bad, bad, that's oo, that's oo! Doo doo doo, that's me, that's me." I was a self-righteous moralist at the age of two or three. I was singing the "B-I-B-L-E, Yes, that's the book for me."*
>
> *I got a firm and accurate idea of right and wrong from being born into a Protestant family. I couldn't convert my dad and make him stop drinking. Our family required loyalty. Now I know children of heavy drinkers have love-hate feelings toward the drinker. Because of my religious convictions, I refused to forgive myself for the hatred which I carefully kept hidden from him. When I was twenty-one my father was killed in an accident. I had lost my father. When I was twenty-five, I had my first breakdown. I despaired of marrying the man I had dated for nine years. I had remained chaste for him.*
>
> *Most of my breakdowns had to do with guilt. Coupled with this was my tendency toward mood swings. I don't know if people who are scrupulous most of the time suffer from a cyclical pattern between depression and elation. I know an attack of exaggerated guilt can put me right into a depression as part of my cycle. When I am elated, I find that bed rest, sleep, and healthy food help me the most. The mind knows how to torture people with bipolar disorder.*
>
> *Once I signed myself into a locked ward because of my bipolar disorder. I felt guilty and abandoned by God. Not until a priest came and heard my confession would I easily behave. I persisted in devotions. Atheistic, humanistic psychiatrists jump on cases like mine and think it proves organized religion guilty of producing mental aberrations. Wrong, wrong, wrong!*

I used to find it necessary to disguise my prayer life on the ward to keep from offending the staff. To me, it was my sign that my mental health was improving. I could pray again!

I think the truly scrupulous person is a victim to the mentality of "You get your pie in the sky when you die." Their life is very death-centered. No relish for the life God has given, no gratitude for his blessings, just shut inside and self-centered. Everyone has life hard. Jesus didn't have it easy. We can't expect better or easier. Only forgiveness helps, and eventually eternal life, unless we reject all three. I hope my input is of value to others.

Finally, one person who was careful to distinguish between her experience of manic depression and scrupulosity wrote:

Scrupulosity has weighed against the lack of trust and confidence to act in a carefree manner. Scrupulosity has served as a restrictive force. In many ways it has shackled my behavior in relationship in marriage and in normal interactions with others. It has stolen joy and peace from me.

Scrupulosity and Panic Disorder

Recently mental health professionals have recognized panic disorder as a separate problem. Effective treatments include therapy and medications. Panic disorder can occur in combination with other problems. A number of people with alcohol problems actually started drinking because it helps to ease the panic. Once they are free of alcohol, therapists may treat the underlying panic disorder. The DSM IV classifies panic disorder and obsessive compulsive disorder as anxiety disorders. Alertness to panic disorder helps counselors see its presence when it is combined with Scrup/OCD.

Panic disorder frequently appears at times of separation or loss. This is evident in the following experience. A forty-nine-year-old homemaker, who is returning to college, wrote:

In addition to scrupulosity, I have panic disorder, which manifested itself after the death of my son by cancer at the age of fourteen. The current research on panic disorder shows a physiological basis. Although my doctor prescribed other medicines, I am now on Xanax. I rarely take it. But I do need to carry the medication with me — just in case.

I grew up in a wonderfully good and morally upright family. I cannot say that my parents were particularly religious. They were good people. Our home environment was peaceful and loving. I never heard my parents fight. They tended to express negative emotions openly.

Although I do go to confession and spiritual direction regularly, I did not begin these practices to treat scrupulosity but rather to grow spiritually. However, I did find that when I began these practices I had to be careful who I went to. The wrong person worsened my problems. I feared face-to-face confessions with priests that I knew.

I have also had counseling in the past but again I did not go into it to treat scrupulosity. I had three children in rapid succession in my early twenties and I needed counseling.

Right now my scrupulosity takes the following form. I feel guilty about mistakes I made raising my children. This affects my relationships with my children and my husband. I feel guilt when I try to do something for myself, such as returning to college. Some members of my family reinforce my guilt. I also feel guilty because I have let some of my religious practices slide. Morally I have a sensitive conscience, and this seems to bother some members of my family as well.

A fifty-four-year-old woman who has suffered from phobias wrote the following:

My scrupulosity is a little bit better, but still everyday I feel I have committed some sins. I see sin everywhere and in almost everything I do, talk about, or see. I am not cured. I am always afraid that anything or almost anything I do or say or think is sinful. Spiritual direction and therapy have helped me a great deal. Medication has helped a little.

A thirty-eight-year-old artist from Montreal wrote:

I worry about mortal sins. My beliefs on birth control, which go against what our religion teaches, were a problem for me. Now that my two children are thirteen and fourteen, I worry

*what to tell them. I don't want to pass on these beliefs but I
don't want my kids going to hell, either.*

*Scrupulosity has affected my life by making me have a
problem with my thinking. I used to worry that many of
my daily actions were sinful. To calm my doubts I'd see a
priest. Shortly after my marriage and having my children I
began to have panic attacks. I felt so closed in, and then I
developed agoraphobia, which interfered with my children
and husband. I found help and I now lead a self-help group
for agoraphobics.*

*Has scrupulosity helped? Scrupulosity helps me fear God's
punishment. It helps keep me in touch with God and religion. I may have gotten into a whole lot of trouble if I hadn't
worried about sin and eternal punishment. It's also helped
in that it has forced me to look for solutions and contact
people for help. I was always very shy, but my search has
helped me share my problems with strangers and feel braver
toward people.*

Scrupulosity and Anorexia

In the professional literature researchers have noted the co-
appearance of obsessive compulsive disorder and eating disorders.
The OCD Foundation has printed articles on the co-appearance
of these disorders in its newsletter.

As we saw in chapter 3 Scrup/OCD and anorexia together
often afflict women. In centuries past strict fasting laws encouraged anorexia. Young women obtained fame and attention
through fasting. Today our culture emphasizes slimness — not
holiness — and anorexia frequently occurs in combination with
perfectionism and an achievement orientation.

A forty-five-year-old married female who works as a teacher
reported,

*I spent $35,000 last summer at an inpatient treatment cen-
ter. They helped me a lot. I suffer from anorexia nervosa. I
also suffer from religious scrupulosity. I try to be perfect. My
scrupulosity turned into a mild case of obsessive compulsive
disorder. Staying away from religion helps me control my*

problem. Confession drives me crazy. My psychiatrist, who is also a priest, told me to stay away from church activities. I never try to think about religion. It hurts to do so.

Confession and spiritual direction made my scrupulosity worse, but therapy helped. With medication, there was no change, but now I am unable to take medicine because of other health problems. Religion sets it off. Religion tries to make you perfect. Is this a chemical brain disorder?

Scrupulosity and Alcohol

Alcohol problems confuse experienced therapists. Alcohol problems may initially appear as depression, family problems, marital problems, or vocational problems — and the presenting problem is actually a smokescreen for the real difficulty: the person's total inability to control drinking. Effective treatment requires total abstinence from alcohol. Of course, there are also complex situations where there can be alcohol *and* depression, alcohol *and* phobias, alcohol *and* an intolerable employment situation. These latter instances may be more difficult to treat.

Scrup/OCD and alcohol abuse combine in complex ways. Some respondents affirmed that their primary problem was drinking and scrupulosity was secondary. Some thought the reverse. Others said that even when treatment freed them of alcohol problems, Scrup/OCD remained. These self-reports provide valuable information for anyone hoping to learn more about the relationship between scrupulosity and alcohol.

A forty-eight-year-old nurse reported being helped "by a trustworthy priest I met in AA." She reported she had been able to maintain her sobriety. She grew up in a family where, she said, "my father was a functional alcoholic, but he was always a good provider. My mother also drank and was very unhappy."

She was very neat and the house always had to be in order. This individual was in religious life during her early twenties, left and married, and then divorced. Although treatment resolved her alcohol problem, scrupulosity remained. She worries about making mistakes: "I especially worry about lying or cheating anyone. It drives me crazy if I can't be 100 percent honest. I am trying to give myself a little more slack." She reported being helped by her Twelve Step spiritual program.

One person acknowledged that he drank too much, but also continues to suffer from some scrupulosity at the age of sixty-two. The scrupulosity takes the form of "worrying whether I told my sins correctly or not, or if I did, if God forgave them. I also worry if I was too easy on myself."

Another respondent, a twenty-seven-year-old female, described how she thought alcohol was a symptom of a more basic problem of scrupulosity and obsessive compulsive behavior. She reported that she viewed the alcohol problem as secondary and situational and noted, "I am pretty sure that I wasn't a true alcoholic. I have OCD and dwelled on alcohol during a stressful time." She continued:

> Right now my scrupulous behavior is really not that much. I have overcome most of my scruples thanks to a great confessor, SA, and of course Him whose spirit is behind all the help in the first place. I'm still dealing with some emotional problems that I consider related to scrupulosity, mainly obsessive compulsive behaviors.
>
> I grew up as an only child of parents who were in their mid-thirties at the time when I was born. They had some trouble conceiving and they wanted to have more children. Because of birth complications, the doctors told my mother to stop having children. My parents valued me greatly. My father provided well but worried about money. He finds it hard to communicate with people, especially my mother. Sometimes, especially when stressed, he abused alcohol. He bottles up emotions like rage, and then blows up. I learned to mediate. For many years, I pleased others at school and work. I disliked conflict. I had panic attacks in angry situations.
>
> I'm saying negatives about my family because I think they might have contributed to my scrupulosity. Positive things balanced them out also. I could tell that when they acted in anger it was because they weren't able to act calmer. Over the years this has led to forgiveness and understanding.
>
> I've been in therapy a couple of times but not specifically for scrupulosity. The first time I saw a counselor for some

interpersonal problems. She lacked experience. I was in a deep depression and kept going downhill fast. That's when I was abusing alcohol, and shortly afterward I checked myself into an alcohol rehab program. This lasted for a month and the counselor there was tougher on me but also did me more good.

Through my life there have been changes in my scrupulosity. Even the downs have never been as severe as they were before I met my confessor. My bad scruples surfaced during late high school and early college times. Religious and mortal issues hit me with force. I fought with my mother. She said college was stealing my moral standards. I feel my scruples were an unconscious playing out of this conflict.

My problem with alcohol abuse has also caused some changes. I acknowledge my lifelong perfectionism. I still blunder and even commit mortal sins. But I rely more on God and less on myself to keep me from temptation. Having screwed up big time in life I can distinguish between this and scruples.

I'd like answers to these questions. How is scrupulosity related to OCD? How is OCD related to other emotional problems? How does alcohol addiction relate to these? What role did my family play? I'm learning answers to these questions by going to Adult Children of Alcoholics support groups.

A thirty-year-old female wrote:

God has healed much of my scrupulosity and obsessive/ compulsiveness through AA. Years of obedience to a priest have helped me. I had difficulty surrendering to him. I am now a different person than I was ten years ago.

Another respondent reported that even after he stopped drinking and began attending treatment regularly, his scrupulosity remained. He stated:

I am an alcoholic and have been in AA for sixteen years and have not had anything to drink in sixteen years. I also suffered from depression afterward and went to different psychiatrists, but they didn't help. And all along I was go-

ing to see priest after priest. I didn't get better. Then all of a sudden, five years ago, my business got worse. I used to go to confession two or even three times each week. Believe me, it was torment. Suddenly Jesus sent me to a priest who cared. He truly cared, and would listen. He would recommend. He would tolerate a complete and detailed confession, no matter how long it took. Eventually after many confessions and about two years I began to feel better. I am now, at age forty-eight, better than I have ever been in my life.

Scrupulosity and Homosexuality

Psychiatrists no longer consider homosexuality to be an emotional problem. However, Scrup/OCD and homosexuality together can evoke intense isolation and loneliness.

A fifty-two-year-old male wrote: "Where's the church when you need her?" This respondent noted that "obsessive compulsive behavior makes daily life a living hell and a nightmare. Freud stated that his sickest patients couldn't invent OCD. In reading this, I realized how troubled I was."

For this respondent, confession produced no change, but spiritual direction was helpful. He reported that scrupulosity has had a very severe effect in all spheres of life. He noted: "To be both scrupulous and gay is to live an insane life. Much harm is done in the name of religion. It's only about a year since I stepped out of scruples. I'm constantly wary to keep them out of my life.

A respondent who is a priest wrote:

My scrupulosity is a bad defense against homosexuality. While away from the church, I was in the gay life and continued to feel its pull even after returning to the faith. When I sinned against chastity, scrupulosity returned.

Scrupulosity has helped to humble me by forcing me to seek the direction and guidance of another. I openly acknowledge problems with homosexuality and scrupulosity. I hope that it has made me more compassionate and sensitive as well as more appreciative of God's mercy.

Scrupulosity and Schizophrenia

Mental health professionals consider schizophrenia to be a crippling problem. However, its intensity varies. Research suggests that about one-third of those who have schizophrenia have one serious episode and then function well. Another group has periodic episodes but is able to function between the episodes. Still another group suffers chronically and needs assistance to function.

Symptoms of schizophrenia include auditory and visual hallucinations, social withdrawal, and the performance of strange and peculiar actions.

Only a small number of respondents in the survey acknowledged suffering from schizophrenia. Their presence is noteworthy, however, because it enables us to observe first the different levels in functioning when the illness is in remission as opposed to active episodes; second, that persons who struggle from this disorder may also have a secondary problem of scrupulosity; third, that nonmedical therapists should refer to competent psychiatrists when needed.

A forty-seven-year-old unmarried female on disability wrote:

I go to confession when I feel the need to go. I see a psychiatrist every four to six months. I take medication daily. The psychiatrist has diagnosed me as paranoid schizophrenic. The priest who counseled me said I was obsessive compulsive. I have had electro-convulsive therapy three times in my life. I am now on five pills a day. Sometimes I take a sleeping pill. A priest used to counsel me about scrupulosity. Right now medication helps. At other times, it stops helping and my doctor adjusts it.

My scrupulosity first appeared when I was in my teens. I was dating a young man and always feared that we would commit a mortal sin. We never did, though. We married. I found out that he didn't want any children. So I divorced him and got an annulment in the church. A few years later my scrupulosity disappeared and I married a man outside the church. Then I divorced this man also as he was a compulsive gambler and he beat me.

My father's death magnified my scrupulosity. Now I know

*I'm going to die too. I know I'll have to pay for my sins. I'm
just sorry I wasn't a better person.*

Despite this suffering, this respondent noted, "Scrupulosity has
kept me from being worse than I already am. Scrupulosity has
kept me from a life of sin. I try to think before I act. I try to be
perfect but I fall short because of that goal."

Another respondent, a middle-aged man from Asia, wrote:

*I was diagnosed as a schizophrenic twelve years ago. In gen-
eral I've done very poorly. However, I have a new doctor
who has prescribed a new medication and I have some hope.*

*When I have an attack of schizophrenia, there's no way of
putting down my self-condemnation. First there's a vacuum,
then a frustration, and then despair. I think that nothing can save me from the despairing thoughts. One of my
consolations is that I am able to write a journal for my
doctor.*

*The bishop exempted me from Sunday Mass. I'm just too
sick to go to Mass because of my preoccupations. I prefer
living life instead of praying too much.*

Scrupulosity and Parkinson's Disease

Many victims of brain damage trauma or illnesses of brain
deterioration that can accompany aging display obsessive compulsive behaviors. Yet research linking OCD to these problems is
sparse.[35] One survey respondent wrote:

*I would suggest that you add Parkinson's, Alzheimer's, and
other central nervous system disorders to your study. I think
you may find a correlation. Today I'm a Parkinson's disease victim and I'm in the mild stages of the progression.
I have nightmares and delusions or hallucinations, all connected with the fear of God. I believe that God no longer
cares for me and that he sends the devil to torment me and
that I will go to hell when I die. I take a medication to offset
the nightmares and delusions.*

*My husband said I have been scrupulous all my life. We've
been married forty-five years. I think scrupulosity can be*

controlled, not cured. My scrupulosity has taken the form about being worrisome about sex and confession. The best time of my life occurred when I was pregnant and my children were young. I was too busy to be scrupulous.

The letter above is remarkable because it was written by the woman's husband. He stated:

Because my wife is unable to write due to Parkinson's disease I filled out your questionnaire based on forty-five years of living with a scrupulous person. I worked with her all these years and know the agony she went through and is still suffering. I hope that I've helped her by being present to her and by getting and reading to her everything I can find on this topic.

I believe the two most troublesome items for her were sex and confession. The worst time of the year was the Lenten season. The worst day of the year was Good Friday. The worst day of every week was Saturday from awakening until after she went to confession at 3:00 p.m. Most often she went twice a month. She went to Communion every Sunday.

It's difficult remembering the last forty-five years but I believe from what she told me of her childhood that she was made this way. Her parents, the good nuns, and one missionary priest put fear into her or didn't realize she was this way.

Ours was a wartime marriage. I was in the army and didn't realize how bad the scrupulosity was until after our third son was born. I guess the scrupulosity was in remission due to our happiness with the kids and our love and respect for each other. But the fear of sin was always looking over her shoulder.

We recovered from this interlude of serious scrupulosity when my wife became pregnant with our fourth child. The recovery lasted twenty years until our fifth child was in high school. Then the scrupulosity came back.

Everything fell apart when I was fired after thirty-five years on the job. A year later our son-in-law died at a young age. Shortly thereafter my wife's sister died. This much stress triggered a new bout of scrupulosity.

*My wife's confessor referred her to a psychologist, who
eventually referred her to a psychiatrist for medication. This
physician suspected Parkinson's disease, and a neurologist
confirmed the diagnosis. He put her on a medicine she
couldn't tolerate, and she went to a psychiatric ward for
eighteen days and went through hell with nightmares and
delusions about bad guys coming to get her and thoughts
about the devil making her drink formaldehyde.*

*I can only tell you part of the story, but I could write a
book if I knew how. I want to help in your study so that
maybe someday the poor souls like my wife can get some
help to overcome scrupulosity. I think a chemical imbalance
is the root cause, aggravated by Jansenistic heresy taught by
the scrupulous priests and nuns in the Catholic Church and
probably by the fundamentalists of other religions.*

Please note. I am a practical and practicing Catholic.

A Special Sadness

Sometimes people suffer so greatly that even the best care and
treatment cannot heal their torment. I received the following letter from a woman whose husband suffered from severe depression
and scrupulosity. I have chosen to include it in this chapter because it signifies an excruciatingly intense level of pain. I would
like to remind readers that research on suicide and Catholics suggests that practicing Catholics generally face a lower suicide risk
than others. Thus the following letter offers the reader a view of
scrupulosity and other problems at their most hopeless level. A
reader writes:

*My husband received the little Scrupulous Anonymous news-
letter for years before his death. Since then they have continued to come and I find them very interesting.*

*Your questionnaire arrived in the last issue. I decided to
send it back, answering as I believe my late husband would
have done. I hope this helps your research.*

*My husband's psychological problems took the following
forms. He suffered low self-esteem despite praise by others.*

Negative thoughts constantly plagued him. He felt guilty and unworthy even while serving weekday Mass.

He grew up in a poor family with an alcoholic father who died early. He resented the heavy responsibility of caring for his mother. Unable to go to college himself, he put his youngest brother through college. He always felt guilty about his resentment over life's dealings.

He worked as a carpenter — a good one. My husband was a wonderful person, and a good father and husband until his retirement. Then his scrupulous tendencies gradually became worse and led to depression that became more and more severe as he grew older. He was hospitalized many times, had so much psychiatric therapy and medication, and even shock treatments. Temporary improvements always led to more severe depression.

After six suicide attempts, he finally succeeded. While in a locked ward, he hung himself. Finally he was free of the hell and torture of eight years of depression so severe it is difficult to understand. His wonderful grown-up children and I accepted the peace he'd found — freedom from his tortured mind — but he is greatly missed. We cling to the many happy years and good memories and thank God for them, and pray every day for him.

Chapter 10

DIAGNOSING SCRUPULOSITY, OCD, AND OTHER PROBLEMS

How do mental health professionals diagnose scrupulosity? What treatments help? I hope this chapter helps people with Scrup/OCD understand their condition better. I hope it helps professionals understand this problem with more clarity. Perhaps this chapter can provide comfort and encouragement to those who have avoided seeking help. Others with Scrup/OCD want to be informed consumers, and this chapter is also designed to help them do this.

People with Scrup/OCD puzzle many therapists. Psychologists, psychiatrists, and other professional helpers need to know what questions to ask about Scrup/OCD.

For clergy and other pastoral workers, the ideas in this chapter can help them to decide when to treat a person themselves and when to refer that person to other professionals.

A person with Scrup/OCD may desire a professional who has experience in treating Scrup/OCD. Unfortunately, such a person may be hard to find. The next best thing is a professional with experience in treating OCD. Along with this, a sensitivity to religious issues is required on the part of the professional. The OCD Foundation provides a list of professionals who indicate an interest in treating OCD, but the foundation does not screen these workers for competence. Rather, the therapists themselves have completed a form indicating their interest in treating OCD. (Write the OCD Foundation, P.O. Box 70, Milford, CT 06460.) Finding a physician with the expertise to treat Scrup/OCD may be easy or may be difficult depending on where you live.

Many people with Scrup/OCD respond well to medications. A new specialty has emerged within psychiatry. There are now physicians called psychopharmacologists. They specialize in prescribing medication for emotional problems rather than being therapists. Despite suggestions to the contrary, I think prescribing proper medication for Scrup/OCD can be very complex.

Making the Diagnosis: Employing the Mental Status Exam

Mental health writers have criticized the idea of diagnosis. Thomas Szaz even suggests that mental illness is a myth. A sad fact remains. The lack of recognition of Scrup/OCD has robbed sufferers of effective care and treatment. Countless survey respondents echoed their anguish. They suffered silently and alone. By recognizing Scrup/OCD, we professionals can reach out and be helpful.

The initial task of the mental health professional dealing with a referral of scrupulosity or obsessive compulsive disorder is to understand its presence and ramifications. Diagnosis can be made using the mental status examination (see Cohen 1995), which includes questions in twenty areas of emotional functioning. In its current form, the mental status exam may overlook Scrup/OCD. Professionals need to remember: if you don't ask something, the patient won't tell you. Good mental status exams identify other psychiatric problems that accompany Scrup/OCD.

DSM IV, published by the American Psychiatric Association, lists criteria for OCD and other problems. Mental health professionals need to be well-versed in the DSM IV. Major bookstores and reference sections of public libraries carry this book.

Asking about Obsessive Compulsive Disorder

Rituals, intrusive thoughts, and a feeling of being out of control characterize OCD. Rituals may include handwashing, checking, contamination fears, or hoarding behaviors. OCD thinking includes disturbing thoughts, fears of losing control, and doubts. People with OCD develop magical thinking. They believe that performing their rituals keeps the bad thoughts away or keeps them from acting badly.

A joke illustrates this. There was a man on a train. He kept tapping his seat, touching the window with his elbow three times,

and snapping his fingers. The conductor said, "What are you doing?" The man said, "I'm afraid the train's going to run into an
elephant." The conductor said, "That's silly. Elephants don't live
around here." The man said, "You're right, sir. That's because
what I'm doing keeps the elephants away."

Mental health professionals need to identify behaviors that accompany disturbing thoughts. People with Scrup/OCD keep these
hidden because of shame and embarrassment. Therapists need to
gently ask questions. Are there things you do to keep bad things
from happening? Do you have thoughts that you wish would
go away? Do you ever clean too much? Do you have any secret habits? Do you have things you have to count in a certain
sequence? Therapists can administer written checklists. These includes the Maudsley Inventory, used in our survey, or the Yale
Obsessive Compulsive Inventory. Sometimes people feel greater
freedom when writing things down rather than talking.

Family members can provide information when the person
seeking help has authorized their involvement. Smiles (or agonized sighs) occur when therapists ask, "Does Ed have any rituals
at home?" or "Does Alice ever insist that the furniture be lined
up a certain way?" Information like this may be too embarrassing
for the person seeking help to offer.

Therapists need to know the difference between obsessive compulsive disorder and obsessive compulsive personality disorder.
The first is described in the previous paragraphs. The second
involves personality traits, including perfectionism, a need to
control others, being meticulous, and stinginess.

Do people with obsessive compulsive disorder (OCD) also have
obsessive compulsive personality disorder (OCPD)? The answer is
sometimes yes and sometimes no. Research studies are mixed on
this issue. Qualities like perfectionism and attention to detail do
not imply Scrup/OCD.

Asking about Scrupulosity

It is important to look for the presence of scrupulosity. Learning
about St. Ignatius, St. Alphonsus, Martin Luther, or St. Veronica can be helpful. Such knowledge helps nonreligious therapists
develop greater empathy toward Scrup/OCD.

The description provided by Father O'Flaherty is helpful to review. First, scruples involve overconcern with one small part of behavior.

Second, people with Scrup/OCD recognize their scruple as a weird or unwanted thought. (Psychoanalytic writers call this ego-dystonic.) People with Scrup/OCD resist acting out on their bad thoughts. (Freud went so far as to say they never do.) This differs from people with impulse control problems who act out.

Third, people with Scrup/OCD feel they commit multiple mortal sins. For Catholics, this requires confession, and unless the confessor is inspired, people with Scrup/OCD stop going. On the other hand, understanding confessors help greatly. Since Vatican II the presence of scrupulosity remains more hidden. The council did not eradicate this problem, and our task of helping people with Scrup/OCD remains.

Fourth, scrupulosity involves doubt. Joseph Ciarrocchi's book describes scrupulosity as "The Doubting Disease."

Fifth, St. Ignatius reminds us that the wrangle of doubts and counterdoubts can provide pleasure. Freud recognized this also. A trap in treatment occurs when therapist and patient enjoy their discussions and avoid facing change.

Sixth, people with Scrup/OCD debate their guilt and innocence in their minds. It never ends.

Seventh, there is doubt over eternal welfare. It takes the form of a blind rush for certitude. In the past, clergy often tried to help stifle this compulsion by command or frightening story. It just doesn't work. Some modern therapists may try to lessen this panic by suggesting the nonexistence of the afterlife. This approach is not effective and may make the scrupulous person wary of the therapist as an outsider who doesn't respect his or her basic beliefs.

Finally, St. Ignatius believed that scruples enter "into a mind which is healthy, normal, and free of pathological disorders." Modern research provides clarification. There are highly functioning people who display OCD. Chapter 4 discusses successful people with Scrup/OCD. It is important for therapists to recognize that Scrup/OCD can be an isolated part of the personality. However, research and stories from our respondents suggest that scrupulosity displays greater complexity than Ignatius realized. As chapter 7 indicated, other serious mental health conditions requiring treatment may be present.

Comorbidity of Scrup/OCD
with Other Disorders

The mental health problem which most frequently accompanies OCD and scrupulosity is depression. Sixty-four percent of respondents noted that depression had accompanied their scrupulosity. For many years a debate has occurred on the relationship between depression and OCD. This concerns depression and Scrup/OCD as well. Is depression the main problem? Is depression expressed as Scrup/OCD? Since early antidepressant drugs helped OCD, some thought healing the depression also cured OCD.

Another theory, now recognized, suggests that the crippling aspects of OCD, the isolation and feeling out of control, create the depression. In this view, depression lifts when OCD is treated. To support this view, researchers note that only some antidepressant drugs alleviate OCD effectively.

I think both explanations can be true. There exists a complex relationship between OCD and depression. Improvement in one area helps in the other.

When working with people who have Scrup/OCD, it is important to look for signs of major depression. These include hopelessness, despondency, low energy, suicidal ideas, changes in appetite or sleep, and lack of pleasure in activities.

Respondents in our survey indicated other mental health problems present with scrupulosity. Getting well means treating all conditions: alcohol problems, phobias and panic disorder, eating disorders, and, in rare cases, schizophrenia. Therapists need to look into all these combinations.

When working with children, additional ideas concerning diagnosis may be helpful. Asking, "Do you ever get really scared about dying and going to hell?" may elicit helpful information. Some further diagnostic possibilities can be reviewed when working with a child referred for Scrup/OCD. Some researchers suggest a relationship between attention deficit hyperactivity disorder, Gilles de la Tourette syndrome, and obsessive compulsive disorder. Looking for the presence and possible combination of all factors is needed for a thorough diagnosis.

Effect of Scrup/OCD on Parents, Spouses, Children, Family

One important and neglected area is how Scrup/OCD has affected significant other people in the person's life. While there are cases where the person with scrupulosity has gone to great lengths to maintain secrecy, it is often much easier to do this in employment or social situations than in family relationships. While one person in the survey noted his condition was between himself "and his Creator" and didn't include his wife, OCD and scrupulosity can have far ranging effects on families and marriages. Some spouses may be able to take the symptoms with a grain of salt. In other marriages, the Scrup/OCD can be devastating. People with Scrup/OCD worry about passing on the malady to their children. A number of articles in the OCD newsletter have focused on "OCD and Motherhood"; it remains yet for a treatise to be composed on how fathers can grapple best with Scrup/OCD.

Information about family functioning can lead to better treatment. Family members often have been unwillingly cast into the roles of "enablers." For example, they provide endless reassurance, and this keeps the Scrup/OCD fueled. Education about Scrup/OCD for family members can help increase the person's chance of recovery.

Summary Regarding Diagnosis

A thorough diagnosis of Scrup/OCD includes the following:

1. Conduct a full mental status examination that will look for the presence of all possible problems. Frequently depression and sometimes other problems may accompany scrupulosity and OCD.

2. Pay special attention to asking about obsessive compulsive behaviors, including rituals and thoughts. Very often, people won't tell you about them unless you ask in a gentle and understanding way.

3. Learn to view scrupulosity "from the inside out." The eight characteristics of scrupulosity as described by St. Ignatius are

helpful, even though the descriptions are nearly five hundred years old.

4. Be especially careful and thorough regarding the possible presence of depression.

5. Look for and rule out any other emotional problems that may be present.

6. Obtain a view of how things are affecting important family members.

Obviously, all these cannot be covered in a thirty-minute session and probably can't be dealt with adequately in a sixty-minute session. It may be helpful for the professional helper to say something like, "This is a tough thing you've been struggling with. You've been unable to figure it out yourself despite the great amount of time you've spent thinking about it. It may take me a little time to fully understand what is going on." Again, such humility stands in respect of the complexity of the problems being treated and adds to rather than detracts from the authority of the helper.

Part Three

HOW IT COULD BE

The last four chapters of this book emphasize hopefulness and describe helpful treatment approaches for scrupulosity and obsessive compulsive disorder. The effectiveness of behavior therapy and medication for OCD is documented throughout the professional literature. However, these measures do not provide full relief in most sufferers, and there are substantial numbers of people who do not respond to these treatments.

This book suggests that the effectiveness of behavior therapy and medication can be enhanced and magnified by combining these approaches with expert talk therapy, knowledge about positive religious practices, and emphasis on healthy spirituality. I hope researchers and funding agencies will develop research designs of greater sophistication that will look at all these factors. The development of new brain imaging procedures may give researchers a helpful tool.

Healthy religious practices emphasizing trust and peacefulness need to be considered in psychological treatments. Chapter 13 provides some appropriate ideas, and chapters 14 and 15 include ideas from Bishop Howard Hubbard and Joseph Cardinal Bernardin.

The last chapter of the book contains my own personal observations and encouragement from a compassionate Catholic bishop.

Finally, the Appendix presents statistical results from our survey of members of the Scrupulous Anonymous group. While I have endeavored to integrate key findings into the text, readers are encouraged to review the material in this appendix. I hope this data encourages other researchers to do more work in learning about scrupulosity and obsessive compulsive disorder.

Chapter 11

CONSUMERS' GUIDE
TO THERAPIES

Persons with Scrup/OCD wonder about how they will find a therapist who can help. To assist them, I will describe a therapist I met while working on this book. Readers will immediately sense her intuitive awareness of issues related to Scrup/OCD. They will recognize the discipline and training that went into her development of Scrup/OCD as a specialty. Following this description of a real-life therapist who has successfully worked with scrupulous people, I will discuss issues that people with Scrup/OCD need to consider when looking for treatment. My identification in this chapter resides especially with the person suffering from Scrup/OCD.

In an increasingly tight financial climate, many therapists take on cases for which they may not be specifically trained. I believe that special knowledge and interest are necessary to heal people who suffer from Scrup/OCD. Lesley Shapiro treats clients at the specialized anxiety and obsessive compulsive disorders clinic at Butler Hospital in Boston, Massachusetts. I met her at the national meeting of the OCD Foundation. Among many professionals offering consultations, she was the only social worker. I think this speaks to her competence at a convention dominated by psychiatrists and psychologists.

Shapiro obtained specialized training in Dr. Gail Steketee's research project on the treatment of obsessive compulsive disorder. Prior to this her professional work included a stint as a Peace Corps volunteer in Africa. How did Shapiro get interested in working with scrupulosity? She stated:

> When I started treating OCD, scrupulosity presented itself
> frequently to me. So I became more interested in learning
> about it. In addition, there wasn't much by way of under-

standing or treatment that distinguished it from regular OCD. The level of suffering that people were experiencing aside from just the regular run-of-the-mill OCD just seemed so painful. Their standards were much more rigid and strict than what a truly healthy religious life consisted of.

I was working in an OCD clinic and was participating in Gail Steketee's research project as a therapist. The study provided behavioral treatment for OCD. It was a controlled study. This meant if people began the study while on medication, they needed to continue on it. Other people received behavior therapy. There were some other nuances as well. Scrupulosity is hard to treat. I've seen many people improve. People who take the most risks gain the most. Risk-taking is one of the hardest things for people with scrupulosity to do.

The biggest thing that I try to do in working with scrupulous people is to help them recognize that their current way of experiencing their religion is really OCD. Until they are freed of their OCD symptoms, it is difficult if not impossible for them to enjoy their religious beliefs and heritage. They make up their own rules. They get consumed with fear and doubt. Eventually they learn that the fear and doubt are not part of their true religion but are a sign of their OCD.

When people start doing the response prevention and the exposure they get clearer about where to draw the line between healthy religion and OCD and scrupulosity. It's helped me to visit with clergy who back up the behavioral approach. They reinforce the need to let go of doubt and fear and scrupulous rituals and to participate in true religious faith.

I've learned from clergy that people predisposed to scrupulosity hang on to outdated religious beliefs. They lack a mature understanding of faith or God or religion. For them, there's a necessary step. It's letting go and developing a more personal faith that helps someone overcome scrupulosity. You can consider this speculative because there is obviously no research supporting it. It helps to speak with the clergy. In the three scrupulosity groups I ran a priest came in and talked about the problem. He was able to shed light on what was going on from a pastoral perspective. People in the groups said these visits were helpful. The groups lasted twelve weeks. People had the opportunity to meet others with scrupulosity — something they had never done, let alone tell anyone else what was going on for them. Each of the twelve groups developed a separate educational component or theme. There were topics like risk-taking, the need for control, perfectionism, and personality traits like black-and-white thinking. (Interview with Lesley Shapiro, January 19, 1996)

Options for Treatment of Scrup/OCD

Most professionals today believe OCD should be treated by medication and behavior therapy.[36] Their belief approaches dogma. Dr. Edna Foa summarizes the overall effects of medication and contrasts its effectiveness with behavior therapy. "With medications about 40 percent of patients benefit," Dr. Foa stated. "The benefit is about 40 percent reduction in symptoms on the average. With behavior therapy, in the short term up to 90 percent of patients benefit. In the long term, 75–80 percent of the patients benefit. It varies depending on how much work the patient does and for how long. Many times, therapy helps so much that it brings them back their life."

According to these figures, it appears that two million OCD sufferers in the U.S.A. may not find relief from behavior therapy. Medication may not help up to three million of these sufferers.[37]

I think the healing of Scrup/OCD must employ behavior therapy, medication, and other sources as well. The minority viewpoint concerning OCD treatment is the psychodynamic viewpoint. A similar approach — relationship therapy — is practiced by Stephen Levenkron. Freud wrote about OCD, and he believed that psychoanalysis was an effective way to treat it. However, proponents have been unable to marshal scientific evidence to support this, stating that it is difficult to measure this therapy. It takes years and involves a complex relationship between patient and therapist. Leon Salzman, who has written knowledgeably about obsessive compulsive disorder since the 1960s, now acknowledges the helpfulness of behavioral and medical treatments, but he continues to emphasize the need for psychotherapy to address the many other issues that exist in the life of someone with

OCD. He does not provide any empirical evidence to support
this assertion, however. It should also be pointed out that research money in past decades has gone solely into medication and
behavioral studies.[38]

Behavioral and medical writers frequently snipe at therapists
who use talk therapy methods. Stephen Levenkron, author of
Obsessive Compulsive Disorders, reported criticism and even
opposition to his book after it was published:

> I'm controversial in OCD circles. It's odd being very ac-
> cepted in eating disorders circles. I threw a book like this
> into this other arena and it was like throwing a gauntlet.
> Everybody feels challenged by it. I talk about OCD as a de-
> fense mechanism. People want to see it as a disease entity. So
> once again we have the politics of psychology.

Levenkron reports that he has treated many cases of people
with OCD successfully. Success involves combining talk therapy
with medication. How does he document this? "My books are
based on my psychotherapist notebooks. They are accounts of the
research that happens in my office."

He remains dismayed at the reactions of many mental health
professionals toward his book:

> The psychopharmacology and behavioral people feel they
> own OCD, and they don't let anybody else in. The result
> is that many good psychodynamic therapists don't even try
> to crash that gate. It's been my experience that you're not in-
> vited because there's a gate that says, "OCD is all chemical
> and sometimes behavioral therapy helps." Many therapists
> don't want to beat their heads against the wall and don't
> want to try to find acceptance in a field that is predisposed
> against them.

Data from our survey suggest that the human elements of
good therapy contribute to healing Scrup/OCD. These elements
include connecting with another person, being required to meet
behavioral demands, and experiencing trust (see also chapter 15).
It appears particularly helpful for people with Scrup/OCD to
express their troublesome ideas and not be judged harshly.

I agree that many talk therapists have failed miserably at treating OCD, a failure I attribute to many complex factors. However,

it does not follow that we should throw out therapies based on talking and relationships. Here I want to review three major therapeutic approaches. I think the best hope for people with Scrup/OCD involves their combination.

Sufferers of Scrup/OCD need to think about this issue. Ineffective long-term therapy can drain finances as efficiently as OCD symptoms drain energy. Proponents of medication offer some enticing data regarding short-term benefits for some but not all OCD sufferers. I hope by reading this book consumers will better arrive at a decision best for them.

Therapists may be shocked to learn that Freud advocated time-limited treatment for sufferers of OCD. He refused to let the Wolf Man babble on forever:

> I determined — but not until trustworthy signs had led me to judge that the right moment had come — that the treatment must be brought to an end at a particular fixed date, no matter how far it had advanced. I was resolved to keep to the date; and eventually the patient came to see that I was in earnest. Under the inexorable pressure of this fixed limit his resistance and his fixation to the illness gave way, and now in a disproportionately short time the analysis produced all the material which made it possible to clear up his inhibitions and remove his symptoms. (Freud 1963, 167)

The Use of Medication

The history of the use of medication with persons with obsessive compulsive disorder is interesting. It appears people with OCD, unlike those suffering from many other conditions, have often been undermedicated rather than overmedicated. Numerous critics caution against or even condemn the overuse of medication for certain conditions including schizophrenia, attention deficit/hyperactivity disorder, and depression.

In the 1950s researchers discovered antidepressant drugs. They included two major classes: tricyclics and MAO inhibitors. Trade names included Tofranil, Elavil, Parnate, and Nardil. Many of these drugs have serious side effects. These include heart problems, effects on major nerves, and other bodily disturbances.

Researchers discovered that one tricyclic, Anafranil, appeared to help depression and OCD simultaneously. Unfortunately, this drug caused the death of some patients because of its cardiac side effects. In addition, Anafranil evokes grand mal seizures in about one out of every 150 people who take it. The FDA refused permission to use this drug in the United States. During the 1970s research accumulated, demonstrating that Anafranil did help OCD. Many people went to Canada or Mexico and smuggled this drug in for their own use, attesting to the anguish and suffering OCD causes ("Brain Wound Eliminates Man's Mental Illness," 12). In 1991, the FDA approved Anafranil, and mental health professionals have since received advertisements touting its usefulness with OCD. According to one pamphlet, "In more than 15 carefully designed research studies with Anafranil, more than 60 percent of the patients with OCD were helped" (CIBA-Geigy 1992, 19).

In the late 1980s doctors began prescribing a new antidepressant — Prozac. In comparison to previous antidepressants, Prozac appears to be a safer drug, at least so far. Short-term studies indicate a lack of serious side effects. Studies by researchers such as Michael Jenike at Harvard University show that Prozac eases OCD symptoms in many people. The FDA has approved Prozac for treating OCD.

A twenty-eight-page pamphlet, *OCD — When a Habit Isn't Just a Habit: A Guide to Obsessive-Compulsive Disorder* is available from CIBA-Geigy (c/o Pharm Ethics Inc., P.O. Box 2001, Pine Brook, NJ 07058). It notes:

> Researchers believe that OCD is linked to an imbalance of a naturally occurring chemical in the brain called serotonin. Serotonin serves as a "bridge" in sending one nerve cell to another. It appears to be involved in regulating repetitive behaviors. The fact that a medication helps people with OCD supports the theory that biochemical factors are involved in OCD. (CIBA-Geigy 1992, 16)

There have been still further advances in medication for OCD. Medications like Zoloft and Paxil work like Prozac.

My conclusions concerning medication and OCD are as follows: First, medication helps a small number of sufferers in an almost miraculous way. Second, a substantial number of people with OCD obtain help from medication. Third, medication does not help huge numbers of OCD sufferers.

I remind readers also of a minority position concerning medication for OCD. Psychiatrist Peter Breggin is a staunch critic of what he considers an inappropriate use of medication for various conditions including OCD. He asserts that empathy and compassion contain unrecognized healing potential regarding OCD and depression (Breggin 1991, 1993).

Agere Contrare: St. Ignatius, William James, and the Cognitive Behaviorists Join Forces

A second approach to dealing with Scrup/OCD is what modern professionals call the cognitive behavioral approach, which asserts that behaviors must change in order for a person to change. Behavior therapists do not talk with a person about childhood events connected to OCD. They identify OCD behaviors and help the person eliminate them.

P. M. Emmelkamp, a researcher in the Netherlands, has reported success in changing OCD behaviors. He has applied the method of "response prevention plus exposure" to many situations involving OCD. This method consists in identifying the compulsive rituals and then gradually helping the person stop them. Emmelkamp noted that it is important to do this gradually rather than suddenly, as illustrated in the following case.

Emmelkamp treated a woman who feared germs and believed the faraway home of her parents bred contamination. She developed washing rituals for whenever she touched an object that she thought might have come from the home of her parents. Even money coming from the direction of her parent's city could evoke terror. She spent most of her time house bound washing her hands and changing her clothes. Emmelkamp asked her to make a list of things she feared, ranking them from least to most. Each week she worked on avoiding rituals in a certain grouping and gradually she confronted her more powerful fears. Within several months she successfully touched and handled objects which earlier had provoked extensive handwashing.

Behavioral psychologists create a climate where the OCD sufferer can confront fears gradually. These therapists tell their clients that getting better requires them to confront difficult and scary situations. The therapist's role is similar to that of coach and support person. Behavioral therapists also enlist the help of spouses, parents, or other family members.

This approach grows out of some of the ideas of William James, notably the "James-Lange" theory of emotion, which states: if you act a certain way, you will start to feel emotions that are consistent with your actions. Thus, if you feel panic and flee, you will continue to feel panic. However, if you feel panic but instead of fleeing take a stand and face the fear, you get stronger.

Dr. Edna Foa treats people with OCD at her outpatient clinic at the University of Pennsylvania Medical College. Critics from around the world acclaim Dr. Foa's book *Stop Obsessing,* a practical guide co-authored with psychologist Reid Wilson that offers suggestions and behavior therapy exercises that can be done at home. Dr. Foa noted:

> We've worked with many people who have religious scruples. Several were Jewish, many were Catholic. One example that comes to mind is of a Jewish woman who was worried whether she was keeping the dietary laws properly. She worried that she might have touched something with milk in it while she was cooking. Or she worried that milk was dripping into the meat. She would continually throw out dishes because she felt they were contaminated. It cost a fortune to keep getting pots and pans because she kept throwing them away, feeling they were not kosher enough.
>
> Some people say prayers over and over. So if praying has become a compulsion, we give them the assignment to always put a mistake into the praying. That way, it is imperfect but still acceptable.

At the clinic, Foa has worked with many cases of scrupulous people troubled by blasphemous images:

> One Roman Catholic patient felt terribly blasphemous and had angry and obscene thoughts about God. These were very upsetting and frequently came to him while he was sitting in church, so he stopped going to church. I worked with his priest, and together we encouraged him to stay with the images until they didn't bother him. He did well and was re-

lieved not to be so tortured and plagued by these thoughts and images.

Foa stated that it is often helpful for behavior therapists to work in conjunction with the clergy:

> I find that priests, ministers, and rabbis can often distinguish OCD because they are aware of what is involved in being a normal religious person. Or a person with OCD will be calling them all the time with questions. It is helpful for a clergy person to work with a behavior therapist. If there is no behavior therapist available, the clergy person could benefit from reading a book such as *Stop Obsessing* and applying the behavioral principles.

Another common religious obsession is fear of the devil. "Exposure therapy helps for this condition," Foa said. "We see a lot of people at the clinic who are afraid of Satan. So we have movies like *The Exorcist*. We let them watch it. It actually works — asking them to do the thing they're most afraid to do."

Foa's experience as a clinician resonates with the experiences of persons with Scrup/OCD who participated in this study and described having problems with confession:

> If patients have excessive anxiety that is diminished by compulsive confession, we don't allow them to go to confession for a while. They have to learn to experience the anxiety without confession. If they are fearful of confession, then we ask them to go and to do so imperfectly — not 100 percent. The idea in general is for them to see that they can be worthy even if they are not perfect.

I asked Dr. Foa how she became interested in working with people with OCD. She stated:

> I was trained as a behavior therapist by Dr. Joseph Wolpe, the founder of behavior therapy. The first patient he gave me in the clinic was a woman suffering from severe OCD who was obsessed with death — she saw cemeteries, wreaths, funeral homes, and other signs of death everywhere, and soon her entire world became so contaminated that she never left home. She was completely housebound. Then she got better, but not immediately. This piqued my interest in OCD.

Foa also noted that behavior therapy has evolved since 1971. "At that time," she said, "we were doing systematic desensitization that really isn't the most effective approach for OCD. We have learned that we really need to use response prevention plus exposure" (Interview with Dr. Edna Foa, December 13, 1995).

St. Ignatius recommended a similar approach, but modern-day behaviorists have added that feared situations should be faced gradually and systematically. In his *Spiritual Exercises* St. Ignatius described his own tendency to develop scruples and obsessive compulsive behavior:

> After I have trodden upon a cross formed by two straws, or after I have thought, said or done some other thing, there comes to me a thought that I have sinned; I feel some uneasiness on the subject inasmuch as I doubt and do not doubt; this is probably a scruple and a temptation suggested by the enemy.

In the *Spiritual Exercises* themselves, St. Ignatius says about scruples:

> The soul that desires to advance in the spiritual life must take a course contrary to that of the enemy. If the enemy seeks to make the conscience lax, he must strive to make it more sensitive, and if the enemy endeavors to make it delicate to excess, the soul must strive to establish itself solidly in moderation so that it may better maintain its tranquility. (St. Ignatius, *Spiritual Exercises,* in Mattola 1964, 138)

Note the similarity to the James-Lange theory.

Vincent O'Flaherty's treatment plan for scrupulosity is very much like that suggested by behavioral and cognitive therapists. It emphasizes facing the scruple and distracting one's attention. O'Flaherty's strategies involve response prevention and exposure. There are four parts to treatment. First, the person makes a list of scruples. Second, the counselor and sufferer review the scruples. They try to better understand the conditions related to the scruples. Third, the counselor teaches the person to reject scruples by becoming involved in distracting activities. Fourth, they develop further strategies to banish scruples in the future. One deficit of O'Flaherty's approach is that it doesn't require the person to rank scruples in order of increasing severity — a listing necessary for successful response prevention plus exposure.

I hope sufferers of Scrup/OCD and therapists who work with them will read O'Flaherty's book, *How to Cure Scruples*. One review in a psychological journal in England noted: "It is encouraging to record that Ignatius of Loyola, Maimonides and modern behavioral therapists are united in their conception of therapy; fears must be confronted and patterns of behavior reversed" (Greenburg, Witztum, and Pisante 1987, 29).

Psychoanalytic Treatment

Psychoanalytic treatment is the minority viewpoint regarding OCD. Freud believed that psychoanalysis could help people with obsessive compulsive disorder. However, as we saw in chapter 1, he recognized that OCD is very complex and suggested that his approaches might have to be modified in the future. Freud even modified his traditional approach when working with his famous patient who displayed Scrup/OCD, the Wolf Man. As noted previously, Freud gave the Wolf Man a specific time that treatment would end. In doing so Freud took control of the therapy in a directive way. Many critics of Freud complain that psychoanalysis with OCD is endless and does more for the bank account of the analyst than the health of the patient. However, Freud himself didn't treat OCD with endless therapy. He has much in common with therapists who set specific time limits on therapy so that the patient will not only talk but will change behaviors.

Just as Christianity as practiced by many Christians does not reflect the teachings of Jesus or the love among the early Christians, psychoanalytic therapy as practiced by therapists is sometimes only a caricature of what was practiced by Freud.

There are good books available describing psychoanalytic therapy, and criticisms of psychoanalysis fill the OCD literature of the past ten years.[39] Here I present suggestions regarding both ineffective and helpful practices in psychoanalytic therapy.

It does not appear helpful for a therapist to allow people with Scrup/OCD to ramble endlessly, to talk about or complain about the same things over and over again, or to otherwise control the sessions. By doing this a therapist runs the risk of maintaining the status quo and continuing the obsessive compulsive behaviors.

A long-term relationship with a trusted and authoritative therapist is a key feature of psychoanalytic therapy. Successful behavior therapists, psychopharmacologists, and spiritual directors who have helped people with Scrup/OCD may have done so because of their own approach, but we should not underestimate the power of a trusting relationship. An active and involved therapist is needed, whatever the theory.

Psychoanalytic therapy should look at how elements of fear, panic, guilt, and despair are related to life experiences, current religious beliefs, and the person of the therapist. A therapist who can direct the therapy beyond these emotions to trust and confidence is essential.

Many people with Scrup/OCD experience a cauldron of conflicting emotions — feelings which may not cause rituals but which may contribute to their severity. A competent psychoanalytic therapist can skillfully identify these complex interactions (Livingston 1989, 12).

There is a form of psychoanalysis called supportive therapy, which emphasizes identifying positive feelings, remembering past experiences of security and love, and creating or reestablishing a network of affirming and helpful relationships. Given the high level of isolation and loneliness experienced by people with Scrup/OCD, these linkages are important. I think psychoanalytic therapists need to follow Freud's suggestion to use goal-oriented and time-limited therapy and to insist upon behavior change as part of therapy.

Heredity, Brain Structure, and Neurochemistry

Many psychiatrists today as well as the OCD Foundation view OCD as a neurobiological disease. They suggest that medication and behavior therapy are the appropriate treatments. In support of this they provide data on the effectiveness of medication in helping OCD. They also present data from sophisticated brain imaging procedures that appear to show changes in serotonin levels in various parts of the brain following medication or behavior therapy. It is intriguing that a psychological therapy such as behavior therapy is now being shown to affect brain chemistry. These researchers imply that advances in medication and behavior therapy will further unlock the mystery of OCD.

However, these individuals do not follow the logic of their own methods to other approaches. This book suggests that a long-term relationship with an effective confessor or counselor can heal OCD symptoms. A large number of survey participants — over 80 percent — indicated that spiritual direction by the right person eased their anguish. It appears to me that before we can rule out the helpfulness of such approaches scientifically, we need to consider applying these brain imaging procedures to people who have been successfully treated with these methods. Such study appears to me to be a further needed step in the scientific investigation of OCD.

Many professionals assert that increased sophistication in our understanding of the brain requires us to abolish the idea of free will. I do not think this needs to be the case. St. Thomas Aquinas provides a paradigm for merging these new scientific discoveries into the Christian conception of free will. St. Thomas suggested that physical properties of the brain itself or injury to the brain could influence free will and in some severe cases eliminate it entirely. However, St. Thomas stood firm in believing in free will, and his philosophy continues to be embraced by the church and some scientists and researchers.[40] While the debate on free will is sure to continue, I think it is important for people with Scrup/OCD and those who work with them to remain open to the view that genetics, biology, family, and environment, and free will all interact and need to be considered in the healing of this condition.

Dr. Jack Sherman, pediatric geneticist at Nassau County Medical Center, New York, has been helpful to me in the past ten years by unlocking genetic puzzles in some of the people I have worked with and referred to him. He graciously reviewed statistical results from the Marist studies on scrupulosity as well as the early twentieth-century data provided by Gemelli. Sherman noted:

The statistics on scrupulosity and obsessive compulsive disorder are very suggestive — almost enticingly suggestive — of a multifactorial genetic disorder. This involves a combination of genes in harmony or disharmony that combines with environmental factors to produce the specific disorder.

There are physical problems which we think have a similar genetic basis. These include scoliosis, hip dislocations, piloric stenosis, cleft lip, and various encephalies. These run in families but without detailed family history it is difficult to make predictions about individuals based on group data.

Dr. Sherman emphasized the potential impact of life experiences in medical and psychological therapies, even in people who have genetically based disorders:

Behavior modification therapies as well as medication appear to be beneficial to obsessive compulsive disorder. I don't think that it's an either/or situation but rather a sage combination. In the future if we are able to isolate the specific combination of genes, then we might be able to reverse some of the damage. However, we still might require combinations of the psychological and medical therapies.

Sherman noted that genetic influences on psychiatric disorders are only rarely traceable to specific genes:

We are onto a couple of genes for schizophrenia. However, the relationship is still not proven. Evidence for specific genes for depression is not very strong. In developmental disorders we have isolated the genetic material for Fragile X Syndrome. We are getting there with the research we keep doing. (Interview with Dr. Jack Sherman, February 12, 1996)

This review by a noted genetic researcher should give pause to those doing research on OCD. The specific genes that may be implicated in OCD are unknown. Life experiences and therapies can interact with a person's genetic capacity. This means that a person with genetic tendencies toward Scrup/OCD should not give up. Genetics does not imply destiny.

Positron Emission Tomography and Scrup/OCD

Research psychiatrist Jeffrey M. Schwartz has pioneered in the use of positive emission tomography (PET) with people who have obsessive compulsive disorder. After performing PET scans on over one thousand subjects, Schwartz reported finding a unique chemical composition in specific parts of the brain in people with OCD. Even more important, he suggests that a form of cognitive behavior therapy can bring about helpful changes in brain chemistry. There are four components to his therapy: relabel, reattribute, refocus, and revalue. These, along with many helpful case examples, are reported in his book *Brain Lock* (1996).

This method of study should prove helpful in the years ahead in testing combinations of short-term and long-term therapy as suggested in this book. It is interesting that Schwartz's philosophy of the person is consistent with that of St. Thomas Aquinas. Both Schwartz and Aquinas emphasize that problems in brain structure or chemistry can lessen the free choice and free will of the human person. Like Aquinas, Schwartz posits the existence of a self independent of brain chemistry, a center of being that makes choices:

> It's not me — it's my brain. Because these thoughts and urges make your life unbearable, you must devise active, positive strategies for working around them. You need to adapt, to keep telling yourself, "It's not me — it's just my brain." (Schwartz 1996)

Scrupulosity and the Internet

Christine Vertullo at Marist College has created a worldwide support group on the Internet for people with OCD. Some of the participants in this global support group suffer from scrupulosity. It is possible to be a member of this group anonymously. My undergraduate class in abnormal psychology has visited this discussion group. These comments from two of my students give some idea of the potential of the support group for people with Scrup/OCD:

> Learning about obsessive compulsive disorders through computer use was a very interesting approach to getting hands-on experience and receiving information about the disorder that no textbook could give a student. I walked away from class with not only more information about the disorder, but also a real sympathy for these sufferers and their families.

Yet it is a relief to know that there is the support out there if these individuals need or want it.

The role of a support group is what I think this Listserve exemplifies to a "T." People can talk about what they are going through, their struggles, and their triumphs, and most importantly someone who can relate to them is reading and responding to it. One thing which really stuck out was the support that people give to others. Even if they can't come up with a word of advice there is always a word of "good luck."

Some Religious Issues in Therapy with Scrup/OCD

Therapists treating Scrup/OCD need to know the religious background of their client. This is unlike fields such as dentistry or heart surgery, where religious attitudes are not relevant.

What happens when the patient is much more religious than the therapist? What happens when religious compulsions center on maybes rather than definites? In general, therapists need to work within the religious belief system of the client. Converting the client to new beliefs is not helpful. Dr. David Greenburg, a British psychiatrist, has worked with persons of the Jewish faith who suffered from Scrup/OCD. He writes:

> The unusual feature of this sort of compulsion is that the patient is not asked to perform tasks that contravene the requirements of Jewish law. It is inappropriate to ask a patient to mix milk and meat, or put non-Kosher meat on utensils, or to refrain from handwashing before a main meal. Even with a knowledge of religious practice, the drawing of boundaries can be difficult, since different communities make differing demands, so that there is a need for careful demarcation between what is neurotic and what is religious for the particular patient.
>
> In general, this distinction concerns risk-taking. The religious person is concerned as to what to do with a utensil in which milk and meat have been mixed, while the obsessive compulsive neurotic is preoccupied that the milk and the meat might have become mixed, and wishes to avoid this by

cleansing rituals and avoidance. (Greenburg, Witztum, and Pisante 1987, 45–46)

Working with Families

Barbara Livingston provides helpful ideas to ease OCD's effect on families: (1) avoid day-to-day comparisons, (2) recognize small improvements, (3) create a supportive environment, (4) set limits but be sensitive to mood, and (5) keep the family routine normal. She writes:

> Often families ask how to "undo" all of the effects of months or years of going along with obsessive compulsive symptoms. For example, to "keep the peace" a husband allowed his wife's contamination fear to prohibit their five children from having any friends in the household. An initial attempt to avoid conflict just grows. Obsessions and compulsions must be contained. It is important that children have friends in their home or that family members use any sink, sit in any chair, etc. Through negotiation and limit setting, family life and "routines" can be preserved. Remember, it is in the sufferer's best interest to tolerate the exposure to fears and to be reminded of others' needs. As they begin to regain function, their wish to be able to do more increases. (Livingston 1989, 12)

Chapter 12

STORIES OF SCRUPULOSITY

The following narratives illustrate the complexity of Scrup/OCD and, as emphasized in previous chapters, show the necessity of being open-minded to all therapeutic and spiritual approaches.

Alone and Sixty-Two

Mrs. J. is a sixty-two-year-old widow, whose husband died two years ago. They shared a happy forty-year marriage and have two grown children who live out of state. She spends hours cleaning everyday. She is compelled to wash any holy object — a rosary or a medal for example — seven times. She believes this keeps her from cursing God.

At various times during her life Mrs. J. became overly concerned about germs. When her children were babies she washed their diapers twice. She remembers her husband kidding her about this. Responsibilities multiplied and as her children got older she reverted to washing their clothes once. In her fifties she went through a six-month period where she cleaned constantly but she eased herself out of this routine as well. She and her husband planned for an active retirement. They bought a camping trailer and dreamed of visiting the Western mountains, but Mr. J. dropped dead from a heart attack as he mowed the lawn.

After her family doctor noticed her raw hands, he discovered the rituals and referred her to a psychiatrist. The psychiatrist always looked closely for depression in older people. He found out that Mrs. J. didn't sleep, had a poor appetite, and had passive thoughts of wanting to die. She cried and told the doctor she did not want to take any medicine. "I don't want drugs. They take away the pain." Mrs. J. was not suicidal and was in good health, except for some dormant heart problems.

The psychiatrist felt stymied. He referred Mrs. J. to a female pastoral counselor at the parish. After seeing the counselor four times, her depression lifted slightly, but she continued the cleaning rituals, which absorbed five hours daily. The pastoral counselor recognized that she was not helping the Scrup/OCD symptoms. Mrs. J. was horrified at thoughts she considered blasphemous, and she cleaned to keep them away. She stopped going to Communion because she felt that she was in a state of mortal sin.

The pastoral counselor knew about OCD. After six more sessions she convinced Mrs. J. to consider taking medication. Mrs. J. returned to the psychiatrist, who considered prescribing Anafranil, but Mrs. J.'s EKG displayed some abnormalities. He chose Prozac instead. Mrs. J. didn't want to take Prozac at first since she remembered reading allegations that Prozac increased hostility. The psychiatrist assured her that Prozac would help her and that he and the pastoral counselor would watch for side effects. To alleviate her fears, he offered to meet with her each week for the next four weeks. He also explained that Prozac was a slow-acting drug and that it would take some time before she started to feel better.

After four weeks she regained some of her old energy. Her angry thoughts toward God abated. She told her pastoral counselor she was spending two hours a day on cleaning rather than six. The pastoral counselor suggested they develop a realistic cleaning plan that took one hour daily. When they did, Mrs. J. discovered that if she cleaned for this hour, angry thoughts toward God did not increase but instead diminished.

The counselor nudged her gently to become active in the community. Instead of cleaning, she spent each morning volunteering as a Foster Grandparent at a local Head Start center. Although the Prozac didn't erase the grief at the loss of her husband, it did give her the ability to stop OCD rituals and get involved with others.

This case illustrates the dramatic improvement some people with Scrup/OCD display after taking appropriate medication. However, Prozac does not eliminate grief and Mrs. J. continued the pastoral counseling.

The Worried Driver

Mr. B. frequently worried that he might have struck or killed pedestrians with his car. Whenever he passed within ten feet of someone, the thought popped into his mind, "Maybe I hit them." To reassure himself, he would retrace his route. Sometimes he continued worrying. To calm these fears, he would buy the newspaper the next day to see if the paper listed any hit-and-run accidents. He was Catholic and believed that it was sinful not to go back and check. A priest's reassurance provided no relief.

Mr. B. was twenty-five years old. He worked in a high-paying job as an accountant. Although he was not married, he had been engaged twice and enjoyed dating. He described his family of origin as "normal." He had two older brothers, and the family history contained no major trauma or psychiatric illness.

Mr. B. went to a psychologist recommended through the Employee Assistance Program at work. They talked about work stresses, but this didn't relieve the need to check. After Mr. B. heard about a behavioral psychologist, he changed to this new therapist. The behavioral psychologist helped Mr. B. list the number of times each day the behavior occurred. They discussed the fact that his urge to check intensified each morning on the way to work. He went back four times each morning to check. The next session took place in Mr. B.'s car on the way to work. The therapist believed in working in the patient's own world.

They worked out a program together. The therapist asked Mr. B. to check three times instead of four. Then the goal would be to reduce the number of checks to two. He would try not to buy newspapers. Mr. B. felt successful after three days and wanted the program to proceed more swiftly. He called his therapist, but the therapist suggested they continue at the pace they had set. Within four weeks Mr. B. was driving to work without checking. This case illustrates the effectiveness of short-term behavioral therapy for some symptoms of Scrup/OCD.

Always in Sin

Mrs. R. is fifty-two years old. She is happily married and has two daughters. In the late 1950s and early 1960s she attended a Catholic school taught by traditional nuns. She made her first confession and Communion when she was eight years old. She remembers being horrified upon reading a pamphlet the sisters gave her before her first confession. It said that to have angry thoughts against God and to consent to them was blasphemy. At that moment, a swear word directed at God popped into her mind. She wasn't sure she consented to it, but because she thought she might have, she mentioned it in her confession. The priest rebuked her. Worse still, he gave her a penance of three rosaries. Everyone else in the class got no more than ten Hail Marys, so Mrs. R. had to stay much longer than anyone else. She felt like the worst sinner in the third grade class. Between the Friday of her first confession and the Saturday of her First Communion some other bad words flashed through her mind. She was terrified that these might mean mortal sin. She considered faking illness to avoid having to go to her First Communion. She made herself go, but afterward felt that she had committed the sin of sacrilege by going to Communion in a state of mortal sin.

During the next four or five years the pattern continued. She confided in no one, and no grown-ups noticed that she was silently suffering. Her bad thoughts multiplied at adolescence. Whenever she had a crush on a boy, she became convinced that she had broken the sixth commandment in a mortal manner. In eighth grade she had a cute male teacher. She convinced herself that because he was married her crush on him violated the ninth commandment. She performed various rituals during adolescence: she had to do her homework in a certain structured manner; she had to put her clothes on a certain way every morning. A special hanger in her closet was designated for the next day's clothes. If she broke any of the sequences, she had to start over.

Since she was a good girl and was on the honor roll, people thought that her periods of withdrawal were simply due to adolescent shyness. They had no idea of all her peculiar rituals. Once she thought of killing herself, which she confessed as a mortal sin. Her teenage years were dreary.

Her family had suffered no major trauma; there was no alcohol or drug abuse. Her parents even had a good marriage. She went away to a secular university. After meeting friends from other backgrounds, she recognized how peculiar and strange all her rituals were. Sometimes they got a little better and sometimes they worsened.

After college she became a reporter for a nationally known newspaper. She wrote wonderful stories, but her managing editor didn't know she wrote her stories after two hours of clothing and make-up rituals. While writing a story on psychoanalysis, she became intrigued and thought that a psychoanalyst could help her. She found a prestigious male analyst, who made it clear that she would be the lucky one if he were to take her on as a patient. She agreed to see him twice a week for at least two years. He told her that the only way to be free from her rituals and sense of sin was to look into childhood for experiences of rage and sexual problems. She was too embarrassed to tell any of her friends about this. In several years she spent enough on therapy to buy a new car. She became increasingly frustrated in the sessions but was told this was due to things that her parents had done to her when she was a little girl. When she was thirty-two, she stopped therapy.

She was cute but discouraged any men who approached her. At thirty-five she met someone she really cared for, and they married and had children. Her husband gave her the space she needed for her rituals but was immensely saddened by her suffering.

When she was forty-six a physician friend who knew about her rituals suggested she consider taking Prozac, which was being prescribed for depression as well as other problems. He referred her to a psychopharmacologist. She was on 20 mg of Prozac for four months, but it had no effect. The doctor increased the dosage to 60 mg and within a month her rituals decreased by 80 percent. For the first time in her life she felt relaxed. She has maintained her gains on 40 mg of Prozac and wouldn't think of going off it. Her husband and children commented that they felt it was like a gift to them to have her be so much happier.

This case illustrates two major points. This women's experiences reflect the stories of many people who remain in therapy with psychoanalytic therapists. Because of the poor fit of the psychoanalytic model, the level of ability of the therapist, or some other reason, money and time are wasted. Second, Mrs. R. is one of a small number of people who dramatically benefit from anti–obsessive compulsive medication.

The Holy Washer

Mr. P., fifty-six years old, suffered from cleaning rituals most of his life. A very conservative Catholic, he held himself to high if not impossible standards of Catholic worship. He never missed a First Friday Mass. He was in the Knights of Columbus and did such a good job there that they awarded him a special sword. His scrupulosity currently took the form of cleaning everything in his house and car three times. He had proposed marriage on two different occasions and both accepted but later broke off the engagement when they discovered that his rituals occupied more than twenty hours each week.

Mr. P. did not trust therapists. He thought most of them had loose morals. A friend of his with marital problems went to a therapist, and the therapist suggested he have an affair. Mr. P. would have nothing to do with therapy. Once his doctor noticed serious skin problems on his hands from washing. The doctor recommended therapy, but instead Mr. P. went to the bargain department store and bought five hundred pairs of latex gloves. His doctor believed him when Mr. P.'s skin improved and Mr. P. told him he had stopped all the cleaning.

At a Holy Name supper, friends introduced him to a beautiful widow; they danced and had fun together. Mr. P. was terrified that his cleaning rituals would scare off the woman he loved. He went to the pastor of the parish, who knew about obsessive compulsive disorder and, in fact, experienced similar problems. He told Mr. P. in no uncertain terms that it was his Christian responsibility to try therapy and provided the name of a behavioral therapist.

The therapist impressed Mr. P. He told him that as a behavior therapist he had a 70 percent success rate working with people with cleaning and contamination obsessions. He told Mr. P. he wouldn't try to talk him out of basic religious practices but would focus on the time-consuming cleaning rituals. He worked with Mr. P. to develop a baseline of situations and times that were spent cleaning. He even visited Mr. P.'s house to get an idea of the realistic requirements of cleaning. Together with Mr. P. he created a program of response prevention and exposure. Little by little, Mr. P. gave up portions of rituals. He and the therapist spent several sessions deciding how to discuss the problem with his fiancée.

After twenty sessions, he was confident he was cleaning his house in a normal way and that it would not interfere with marriage.

The therapist agreed to be available for booster sessions as needed. He cautioned Mr. P. that symptoms could reoccur if he didn't practice his behavior therapy. After two years, Mr. P. was happily married and had kept his Scrup/OCD symptoms under control. He had even given up daily Mass because he liked to cook breakfast for his wife each morning. Needless to say he always did the dishes.

This case illustrates the reluctance of Catholics with scrupulosity to enter therapy. A psychologically sophisticated pastor and a competent behavioral therapist were able to target and alleviate the symptoms. The therapy was so successful that a referral for medication never had to be made.

Doubts over Birth Control

Mr. and Mrs. L. were happily married for twenty years and were raising four children. Four years before they had decided to practice birth control. The house and finances were bursting at the seams. A fifth child would place too much stress on everyone. Both Mr. and Mrs. L. were comfortable with their decision for three years.

Then Mr. L.'s mother and father died within three months of each other, both of cancer. His elder brother was crippled by Lou Gehrig's disease. Mr. L. sank into depression. He couldn't sleep and felt intensely guilty over the birth control decision. He talked to three different priests and got three different answers. One priest lectured him and told him he should stop going to Communion until he and his wife ceased using nonapproved methods of birth control. The second priest told him angrily that the church was out of touch with the modern world and that recent studies indicated that 71 percent of Catholics use birth control. How could God condemn all these people? The third priest just looked sad, told him that this was a difficult situation for many, and suggested that he listen to his conscience. Mr. L.'s doubts wouldn't stop. He made some major mistakes at work because he was so preoccupied. He was a distant lover and knew he left his wife unsatisfied.

His family doctor prescribed Prozac. It didn't help, and he

stopped taking it on his own. He went to a therapist who was highly recommended by the deacon at the parish. The therapist encouraged him to try to live life with its imperfections and to recognize that he and his wife had made a prudent and reasonable decision concerning birth control. He kept doubting and he stayed depressed.

Mr. L. located another therapist, who inquired about his whole life. Mr. L.'s parents had desired to start a clan, and Mr. L. and his wife frustrated this dream by moving away because of a job transfer. Mr. L. devoted himself to his wife, children, and job. This left little time for long-distance commuting to see the grandparents. In therapy, Mr. L. recalled many times when he was a teenager that his mother had told him how important it was for families to remain together. He knew he had let his parents down over the years. Mr. L. yearned to help his brother, but again the long distance made visits difficult. The therapist asked him, "Are there things you could do for your brother without disrupting your whole life?" Mr. L. decided to write two letters each week and to send a video tape of the kids each month. His sister-in-law called him to tell him how much his brother treasured this outreach. During one session, the therapist gently asked, "Can you think of ways you could have met your responsibilities as husband and father and still given your mother the extended family clan she desired?" Mr. L. realized his parents had placed him in an impossible situation. In his heart he knew he would never make a similar request of his children. The therapist encouraged Mr. L. to grieve and explained that intense grief like his might lessen but might not ever go away.

Mr. L.'s depression slowly lifted. He felt less guilty about things he hadn't done for his parents or brother. Surprisingly, his doubts over birth control faded. He became comfortable with the original decision he and his wife made together.

This case illustrates that medications or behavior therapy do not help some Scrup/OCD symptoms. A competent talk therapist identified and discussed guilt-provoking concerns arising from the tapestry of his life. As a result, the doubt and depression dissipated.

Chapter 13

SUGGESTIONS FOR SUFFERERS AND HELPERS

For Sufferers of Scrup/OCD

1. Cardinal O'Connor offers this suggestion for Catholics who suffer from Scrup/OCD:

> I think that a good confessor can be very, very helpful. A good confessor, unless he has extraordinary training, truly extraordinary training, in my judgment, cannot do it all. But if he is a good confessor, he's going to recognize very early in the game what's within his competence and what requires professional help. So I think I could best encourage people by telling them to look for a good, holy confessor, a priest — and then be very honest and recognize that, just as in the practice of medicine, you prevent the cure if you refuse to subject yourself to the prescriptions of the doctor. (Interview with John Cardinal O'Connor, January 23, 1996)

2. Find a good therapist. Many persons with scrupulosity will want a therapist who is competent in treating obsessive compulsive disorder as well as one who is knowledgeable or open to spiritual issues. Asking friends is one way to locate a good therapist. Unfortunately, since many people with scrupulosity have kept their condition hidden, it may be difficult to find a referral through word of mouth. Some therapists who work with OCD may also be competent in working with Scrup/OCD.

The OCD Foundation maintains a list of therapists who show a willingness to work with people with OCD. While there are many competent and helpful therapists on this list, the foundation does not screen them. Other methods of validation should be used to determine the qualifications of therapists obtained from this

150

list for dealing with Scrup/OCD. Ask the therapist, "How many people with OCD or Scrup/OCD have you treated?"[41]

3. For persons with Scrup/OCD, it is important that therapists share similar values. Blatant inconsistencies, such as reported by the respondent who noted "the psychologist said I should go to bed with some gal," are to be avoided.

4. Insurance issues concerning treatment have become more complex. Many managed care contracts for mental health coverage limit mental health sessions to twenty per year. For some persons, there may be a need for more sessions. Managed care has also come under criticism by some persons with OCD and their treating physicians. Some HMOs will not authorize newer SRI (Serotonin Reuptake Inhibitors) medications because these cost more than traditional antidepressants. HMOs may not approve the high dosage levels required for OCD. The complex issues brought up by managed care are addressed by L. Shapiro in her article "Managing Managed Care" (OCD Newsletter, December 1995)

5. Read Stop Obsessing by Dr. Edna Foa and Dr. Reid Wilson.

6. Read The Doubting Disease by Dr. Joseph Ciarrocchi.

7. Join the OCD Foundation, P.O. Box 70, Milford, CT 06460-0070.

8. Join a support group for OCD.

9. Locate a sympathetic priest or pastoral counselor. He or she can provide encouragement.

10. Learn about depression and its effect on OCD.

11. Develop normal religious practices. Scrupulosity takes one small aspect of religious practice and blows it out of proportion. Celebrate religious activities in a normal way.

12. Maintain a sense of humor. Father O'Flaherty suggests that when persons laugh about their scrupulosity, a cure is near.

13. Struggle against perfection. Father Russell Abata, whose book Helps for the Scrupulous, has aided many scrupulous people in the past twenty years, is fond of emphasizing Chesterton's dictum: "Anything worth doing is worth doing...poorly!" Do things humanly. Don't worry about crossing every "t." Take risks. Get moving.

14. Read the book by Dr. David Burns on treating depression. Feeling Good devotes a whole chapter to the crippling aspects of perfectionism. There are helpful exercises in this book.

15. Act against scruples. Church tradition and modern behavior therapy agree: you must face your fears.

16. Exercise and strive for good health. Moderate exercise diminishes scruples.

17. Develop security. I agree with Leon Salzman that insecurity breeds scrupulosity.

18. Postpone scruples. In this way you gain control. Foa and Wilson note:

> If you respond to your obsessions by attempting to get rid of them instantly, to have them gone now and forever, you will probably fail at the task. Instead, take a smaller, more manageable step in order to gain control of one more part of the obsessional process.... The essence of this technique is to stall the obsessions. You decide not to ignore your worries. However, you are going to postpone attending to them for a bit. (Foa and Wilson 1991, 81)

19. Take risks. For many scrupulous people, making a major life decision can awaken even latent scrupulosity. Choice stirs doubts. St. Ignatius knew this; he devoted a chapter of his *Exercises* to this topic. For many scrupulous people, decisions about marrying, moving, retiring, changing jobs, etc. can be almost incapacitating. One way to avoid endless obsessing and doubting is to allow a certain time for reflection, realize that any decision is imperfect and involves risks, and then make the decision.

20. Determine if reading is helpful. As with perhaps no other affliction, scrupulous people have tried to get better by reading books. While many times this may be helpful, on other occasions it may detract from reaching out to human relationships. One respondent said, "In my desperation I turned to books." On the other hand, the printed word has a power to allay doubt. Consider the following:

a. At times scrupulosity arises from doubt. Scrupulous people have a tendency to twist religious ideas. For example, in the one-hour fast before Communion: does putting on lipstick count as food? What about toothpaste?

For some, reading about and reviewing the original idea that has been distorted is helpful. Perhaps one reason for the success of Scrupulous Anonymous is that is reaffirms basic healthy ideas about the Catholic faith in tangible print.

SPECIFIC SUGGESTIONS FOR SUFFERERS AND HELPERS

Older catechisms fostered scrupulosity. The *Catechism of the Catholic Church* of 1994 is more helpful. Father Thomas Santa, advisor to Scrupulous Anonymous, notes that he always keeps a copy of this catechism nearby when responding to questions raised by scrupulous people. Perhaps many of them would benefit from reviewing the source of their scruples and seeing their beliefs in a realistic light.

b. For some, reading books is a way to avoid relationship problems. If this is so, face these through therapy. For other scrupulous people, spiritual reading can represent greater religious maturity, a move toward peacefulness, the spirit of God, and healing. These writers may be helpful: Thomas Aquinas, St. Augustine, G. K. Chesterton, C. S. Lewis, Thomas Merton, Scott Peck, the documents of Vatican II, Eugene Kennedy, Joseph Girzone, John Powell, Norman Vincent Peale, and St. Ignatius.

c. For some the Bible creates scruples. For others, it talks of God's love throughout history, Christ's compassion, and the Holy Spirit's encouragement. These heal scrupulosity.

d. Some survey respondents reported that books on Twelve Step programs helped them. Others reported receiving help from books on dysfunctional families. Scruples serve as a smokescreen for family problems in some people. Readings like these shift the battle to its proper arena.

Some words by Leon Salzman may be helpful in considering the usefulness of books:

> Philosophizing can often provide the way to avoid action and to forgo decision. While it may be a prelude to action, philosophizing often becomes a substitute for living, rather than a design for better living.... Philosophizing provided the impetus for the growth of many seminal ideas in the sciences as well as in the arts. Aristotle, Plato, Descartes, Marx, Whitehead, and many other intellectual giants broadened the horizons of man in many directions. For the obsessive, however, philosophizing becomes perverted into a justification for inaction and a demonstration of infallibility.... The preoccupation with the most minute elements of experience, when examined in a formal fashion, has been the source of profound advances in man's enlightenment, but it can also be a justification for inaction. (Salzman 1994, 28–29)

21. Join an OCD discussion on the Internet. (See p. 201 for Internet addresses.) Scrupulosity causes isolation. One man kept his scrupulosity from his wife for twenty years. To remain anonymous, many people with Scrup/OCD travel to other parishes.

22. Review your life for major errors which may have gone unrecognized due to scrupulosity. Resolve real guilt and make amends.

23. Transcend Scrup/OCD and invest in new time. Recognize the sadness of lost time. Experience the challenge of greater freedom in the future.

24. Help others and do so gently.

25. Learn to pray to "the greatest lover and greatest forgiver." Read Bishop Hubbard's prayer (see below p. 177). Absorb the tone in Maryanne Williamson's *Illuminata*.

26. Become immersed in positive life plans, and practice *Age quod agis* (see above p. 8).

27. Reflect on these words of John Henry Cardinal Newman, suggested by Mother Teresa for readers of this book (correspondence with Mother Teresa, March 27, 1996)

> Dear Lord, help me to spread thy fragrance everywhere I go. Flood my soul with thy spirit and life.
>
> Penetrate and possess my whole being so utterly that all my life may only be a radiance of Thine. Shine through me, and be so in me that every soul I come in contact with may feel Thy presence in my soul.
>
> Let them look up and see no longer me — but only Thee, O Lord! Stay with me, and then I shall begin to shine as Thou shinest; so to shine as to be a light to others.
>
> The light, O Lord, will be all from Thee; None of it will be mine; it will be Thou, shining on others through me.
>
> Let me thus praise Thee in the way Thou dost love best, by shining on those around me.
>
> Let me preach Thee without preaching, not by words but by my example, by the catching force, the sympathetic influence of what I do, the evident fulness of the love my heart bears to Thee.

For Helpers

1. Learn about scrupulosity. Consider it an expression of religious culture. Approach those who suffer from it with the same openness as you would any racial or cultural group. Read. Attend services.

2. Develop a willingness to work with the clergy. The clergy can teach the specifics to therapists unschooled in religious philosophies.

3. Don't judge religious behaviors at face value. Something may appear pathological just because it's different from what prevails in our culture.

4. Learn about obsessive compulsive disorder.

5. Learn about medications for obsessive compulsive disorder. Obtain an understanding of medications your counselees may be taking. Know the side effects, especially the toxic ones.

6. Establish boundaries for your own professional role:

a. Physicians: How much time will you spend reviewing symptoms and quality of life? How will you rate the efficacy of medication? Will you meet family members? Will you encourage patients to obtain behavior therapy or other psychological therapy?

b. Clergy and pastoral counselors: How will you draw the line on when to counsel and when to refer out? How will you look for other emotional problems? How will you locate and evaluate other mental health professionals?

c. Psychologists and other therapists: What treatment model will you use? Are you comfortable with this model? How will you determine when to refer for medication? How will you explain the limits of treatment to patients?

7. Approach the disorder of Scrup/OCD with humility but hope. Despite current psychiatric dogma, no single therapy heals all those who exhibit symptoms. This book has tried to show that a combination of various approaches may be required.

8. Try to diminish OCD behaviors and thoughts. In themselves they can be serious problems.

9. Be open to the possibility that a patient's fearful perceptions from childhood may have been transferred to religion. Effective talk therapy may augment behavioral strategies.

10. Be a compassionate but directive authority figure. Along

with understanding, people with Scrup/OCD need direction and guidance from their therapist.

11. Admit the mistakes you make. This frees the person with Scrup/OCD similarly to admit mistakes and to learn to forgive them.

12. Expand your office to encompass your patient's world. Behavior therapists recognize the necessity of providing active coaching directly in fearful situations. You may need to go to church with your patient to see his or her terror unfold. You may need to make a home visit to pinpoint the effect of Scrup/OCD on other family members.

13. Do a genogram or family tree. Whether genetic, structural, chemical, or learned, depression and Scrup/OCD appear to run in families.

14. Actively seek out other family members during the initial interview. They often provide information you can't get by any other way.

15. Learn about the religious tradition of people with Scrup/ OCD. If they are Orthodox Jewish, read the books of the Torah and understand ancient dietary laws. If they are Catholic, read the new *Catechism of the Catholic Church*. If they are Muslim, read the Koran and learn about the importance of repetitive prayers and other rituals.

16. Be as ecumenical in professional readings as you expect others to be toward religious beliefs.

17. Despite its suggested obsolescence, understand transference.[42] You may discover that patients respond toward religion and you in the way they reacted toward their parents and siblings.

18. Be wary of suggesting to people with Scrup/OCD that they break their own moral codes. Many survey respondents wrote of leaving therapists who encouraged sexual promiscuity. There is no evidence that this heals scrupulosity.[43]

19. Be hopeful, but don't guarantee a cure. The person with Scrup/OCD must do significant amounts of work alone. Be alert to side effects of your theoretical view. Explain these to your patient. For example, response prevention and exposure might increase a person's daily anxiety level. Final exam time might not be an appropriate time to begin such therapy. Psychodynamic therapy might increase awareness of negative feelings toward a spouse or other family members. Provide your patient with a chance

to be an informed consumer. This is crucial when prescribing medication.

20. Be alert to the role of rejection experiences, past and present, in the life of the person who has Scrup/OCD. As Cardinal O'Connor notes:

> It's remarkably worthwhile for counselors to deal with rejection. In my experience of more than fifty years as a priest, and a lot of that with a clinical psychology background, I have found that the most difficult of all problems to live with and the most difficult to manage is the problem of real or perceived rejection — one so severe that all sense of intrinsic worth is destroyed. I think that scrupulosity is often rooted in this. (Interview with John Cardinal O'Connor, January 23, 1996)

Healthy Spirituality

Eliminating religious practices does not cure scrupulosity. For people with Scrup/OCD, a goal must be to alleviate their symptoms and help them create a life with healthy spiritual practices. Thomas Aquinas defined religion as "the virtue of proper relationships." Since people with Scrup/OCD tend to go overboard in their religious life, they need guidance to strike a balance. A problem arises, however, since priests, ministers, or other pastoral workers often lack the training required to work with Scrup/OCD. Most therapists lack understanding of the complex tradition of Catholicism that helps generate Scrup/OCD among Catholics. Most therapists also lack detailed knowledge of other backgrounds that have engendered scrupulosity, including: various Protestant groups, Orthodox Judaism, and the Muslim faith.

I hope this book encourages pastoral workers to learn and practice approaches that help people with Scrup/OCD. This may require further reading, workshop attendance, supervision, and even further education. I hope that mental health workers, especially psychiatrists, psychologists, and social workers, will devote time and energy to understanding the particular religious background of their client. This might involve learning the religious laws, reading inspired works, attending a service, and talking

with members of that faith. Since many people with Scrup/OCD
have problems in church or receiving the sacraments, visiting the
religious milieu provides an extra dimension of knowledge for the
therapist.

When dealing with other problems, therapists have often immersed themselves in the cultural or family milieu of their patients. Salvador Minuchin succeeded in helping people who suffered the trauma of inner city life. He took the risk of traveling to
see them on their turf. His book *Families of the Slums* is a model
of concern and outreach. Many therapists working in early inter-
vention programs understand the need to give service in the home
and community rather than their office. First-hand knowledge of
any situation not only increases empathy but gives therapists the
background to make detailed direct interventions.

Pope John Paul II is concerned about understanding people in
undeveloped third-world countries. Although seventy-five years
old, he is studying several new languages so he can approach
these cultures with first-hand knowledge. This attitude can inspire
therapists as well.

Catechisms and Scrupulosity/OCD

A significant number of survey respondents complained that negative practices in Catholic schooling, fear-oriented threats as
a catechetical style, and a "Baltimore Catechism" or "Betty
Crocker" spirituality emphasizing rules alone crippled their spiritual development and added to their scrupulosity. Since people
with Scrup/OCD are apt to have tunnel vision, their spiritual development often does not include awareness of positive, affirming,
or loving aspects of their faith.

In 1994 Joseph Cardinal Ratzinger approved the publication of
the *Catechism of the Catholic Church*. This eight-hundred-page
book attempts to map out major elements of Catholic belief in
a positive way. Unlike past catechisms, which were limited by
a question and answer format, this book provides a wider and
deeper understanding of what the Catholic Church is all about.
Much of the material is based on the Old and New Testaments,
writings of early Christians, and the thinking of church coun-
cils throughout history. Since many scrupulous Catholics dwell on

limited aspects of their religion, reading this book may help them toward greater spiritual maturity.

Surprises await scrupulous readers as well as people who lack knowledge of Catholicism. With confidence and boldness the book asserts the mercy, grace, and love of a personal Creator. Sections on world religions, immigration and social justice, attitudes toward suicide, and many other areas may startle many readers. The liberal and life-affirming ideas are discordant with many current misconceptions of Catholicism. A cursory review of this book suggests themes of importance to people with Scrup/OCD: God's love, trusting God in every circumstance, Providence, the beauty of the universe, the unsearchable riches of Christ. In the next chapter, "Lilies of the Field," Bishop Howard Hubbard offers application of the catechism to people with Scrup/OCD.

Ten Commandments for Scrupulous People

Scrupulous Anonymous has provided permission to reprint this advice from Father Ernest Miller:

1. You shall not repeat a sin in confession when it has been told in any previous confession, even when there is a doubt that it was told or a doubt that it was told in a sufficiently adequate and complete way.

2. You shall not tell doubtful sins in confession, but only clear and certain ones.

3. You shall not repeat your penance after confession or any of the words of your penance on the score that you had distractions or may not have said the words properly.

4. You shall not worry about breaking your fast before receiving our Lord in Holy Communion unless you actually put food or drink into your mouth and swallow it in the same way that a person does when he or she eats a meal. No hesitations are allowed regarding accidental swallowing of lipstick or skin or such things.

5. You shall not hesitate to look at any crucifix or at any statue in church or at home or elsewhere lest you get bad thoughts

in your mind and imagination. If such thoughts come, they carry no sin whatever.

6. You shall not consider yourself guilty of bad thoughts, desires, or feelings unless you can honestly swear under oath before the all-truthful God that you remember clearly and certainly consenting to them.

7. You shall not disobey your confessor when he tells you never to make another general confession of past sins already previously confessed.

8. You shall believe and act accordingly, so that whenever you are in doubt as to whether or not you are obliged to do or not to do something you can take it for certain that you are not obligated.

9. If, before you perform or omit an act, you are doubtful whether or not it is sinful for you, you shall assume as certain that it is not sinful and shall proceed to act without any dread of sin whatever.

10. You shall put your total trust in Jesus Christ, knowing that he loves you as only God can love and that he will never allow you to lose your soul.

Advice for the Scrupulous

• *Be human not saintly.* People with Scrup/OCD lose sight that perfection kills but doing your best energizes. Too many people with Scrup/OCD try to do everything right or they try to do one small thing perfectly. Both are impossible. The more people try to meet goals like this, the more they will fail.

Therapists can offer feedback when a person with Scrup/OCD crosses the line between worship and *mishagus.* This Jewish term means "silliness." It is an apt term for many things people with Scrup/OCD try to accomplish. Failure is human. People with Scrup/OCD need to learn how to fail gracefully, and often.

• *Make religion one part of a balanced life.* For many, Scrup/OCD symptoms skew their life. When these symptoms abate, it is important not to create more rituals. Therapists can offer suggestions to help clients create a balanced life. For some, it might be better to go to the health club or have breakfast with friends at a diner than to go to Mass every day at 7:00 a.m. For someone trying to be a perfect parishioner, the new priority might be family time in the evenings. Many people with Scrup/OCD suffer loneliness. Camaraderie with friends or connectedness with family provide a healing balm.

Physical exercise, satisfying work, intimacy, family and friendships — time devoted to these and other rewarding activities eases and even cures the depression that accompanies scrupulosity.

• *Enjoy it while you can — read Ecclesiastes.* Scrupulous people strive for perfection, frequently through obsessive work. Qoheleth, author of the Old Testament book Ecclesiastes, warns against workaholism. A biblical scholar provides these insights relevant to scrupulosity:

> The book's insistence on enjoyment is an important voice to be heard by anyone who locates the message of biblical religion more in asceticism than in love and social concern, and who feels that biblical religion in some way militates against enjoyment. Qoheleth's negative assessment of the workaholic should be constructively provocative for those who believe that posture to have value or to be synonymous with religious dedication.
>
> In no way can Qoheleth be said to have had a close personal relationship with God. Not infrequently the rhetoric of the believing community creates the impression that all the faithful should be experiencing such a relationship and that they are at some way at fault if they do not.
>
> Clearly countless thousands of devout people travel in the dark as did Qoheleth, and they can find dignity in the believing community because Qoheleth was deemed worthy to have a place among the biblical writings. Surely the book needs to be complimented by the other voices of scripture, but its voice is of considerable importance. (Wright 1990)

Qoheleth advises scrupulous people:

> The breath in our nostrils is a puff of smoke,
> reason a spark from the beating of our hearts:
> extinguish this and the body turns to ashes,
> and the spirit melts away like the yielding air.

'In time, our name will be forgotten,
nobody will remember what we have done;
our life will pass away like wisps of cloud,
dissolving like the mist
the suns rays drive away
and that its heat dispels.

Come then, let us enjoy the good things of today,
let us use created things with the zest of youth:
take our fill of the dearest wines and perfumes,
on no account forgo flowers of Spring
but crown ourselves with rose buds before they wither,
no meadow excluded from our orgy;
let us leave the signs of our rivalry everywhere,
since this is our portion,
this is our lot.

• *People take precedence.* Involvement with others is generally healthier than the performance of private rituals. The flow
of human interaction provides an arena for response prevention
plus exposure. Being with people, especially enjoying their company and sharing fun with them, is incompatible with peculiar
rituals.

• *Break plans, take risks.* Some people with Scrup/OCD try to
plan not only the rest of their earthly life but their eternal life as
well. This simply can't be done. Our worst suffering comes unex-
pectedly, like a thief in the night. People with Scrup/OCD attain
greater happiness when they are ready to jump into unexpected
opportunities.

• *Smile with God.* In Professor John Scileppi's office at Marist
College, there is a picture of Jesus laughing. This startling por-
trait touches visitors to the office. The bestselling series of books
about Joshua by Father Joseph Girzone depicts a Messiah who
laughs, jokes, and enjoys the good things of creation. These artis-
tic creations differ from the gloomy and frequently depressing
icons from Roman or Gothic artists. Perhaps religious art in the
third millennium will resonate with a happy Creator.

G. K. Chesterton, lover of the human condition as well as
sociability and merriment, offers sufferers of Scrup/OCD this
encouragement:

Joy, which was the small publicity of the pagan, is the gigantic secret of the Christian. And as I close this chaotic volume I open again the strange small book from which all Christianity came; and I am again haunted by a kind of confirmation. The tremendous figure which fills the Gospels towers in this respect, as in every other, above all the thinkers who ever thought themselves tall. His pathos, almost casual. The stoics, ancient and modern, were proud of concealing their tears. He never concealed his tears; he showed them plainly on his open face at any daily sight, such as the far sight of his native city. Yet he concealed something. Solemn supermen and imperial diplomatists are proud of restraining their anger. He never restrained his anger. He flung furniture down the front steps of the Temple, and asked men how they expected to escape the damnation of Hell. Yet he restrained something. I say it with reverence; there was in that shattering personality a thread that must be called shyness. There was something that he hid from all men when he went up a mountain to pray. There was something that he covered constantly by abrupt silence or impetuous isolation. There was one thing that was too great for God to show us when he walked upon our earth; and I have sometimes fancied that it was his mirth. (Chesterton 1965, 211)

One priest recommended that scrupulous people play poker. He pointed out the incompatibility of the fast pace of this game with scrupulous behaviors.

• *Absolve yourself from thoughts and feelings.* Therapy with the warmth of a compassionate therapist provides the acceptance of thoughts and feelings that people with Scrup/OCD recoil from. Whatever the philosophy of the therapist, talking about these distressing feelings eases the pain of Scrup/OCD.

• *Be like someone you admire.* Therapists can ask, "Who do you admire in your religion?" Discussion can offer specific behaviors to be emulated.

• *Approach the Ten Commandments with an awareness of how they affect scrupulous people.*

Throughout the survey respondents provided descriptions of difficulty they experienced with behaviors relating to specific commandments. The following is offered to summarize some of these difficulties.

I. *"You shall worship the Lord your God and Him only shall you serve."*

Because doubt is a characteristic of scrupulosity, some sufferers interpret their doubt as sin. It may help sufferers of Scrup/OCD to remind themselves of this fact. Their doubt may signal OCD or genuine religious strivings, but not doubt in the sense of heresy or schism.

II. *"The name of the Lord is holy."*

This commandment stirs anxiety and a feeling of sin. Intrusive thoughts define Scrup/OCD, but in no way are they sins.

III. *"Remember the Sabbath Day, to keep it Holy."*

Several survey respondents recalled lists of sins from their Baltimore Catechism days. They remembered injunctions against working on Sundays. The new catechism provides a positive outlook on the Sabbath: "The institution of Sunday helps all to be allowed sufficient rest and leisure to cultivate their familial, cultural, social, and religious lives" (*Catechism of the Catholic Church*, 2194).

IV. *"Honor your father and mother."*

We hope there is special grace for people who suffered physical or sexual abuse, neglect, parents with alcohol or drug problems, or other disruptions. When childhood is not a time of security and happy memories, bitterness and anger are natural and understandable reactions. But biological researchers have noted many instances of OCD that are independent of family or marital strife. Blaming parents for OCD symptoms in children is not helpful. Some survey respondents wrote forcefully about their difficult lives as small boys or girls. Such problems do appear to be associated with or to magnify symptoms of Scrup/OCD and depression.

Therapists can help convert doubt over family obligations into realistic goals so that persons with Scrup/OCD can honor their father and mother. Becoming aware of past anger is just one step on the road to being healed, but venting anger often creates more problems.

V. *"You shall not kill."*

Aggressive thoughts bother people with Scrup/OCD. As with the second commandment, they must remember that thoughts are not actions. Bishop Howard Hubbard offers encouragement on this in the last chapter. I know of no cases of persons with Scrup/OCD who have been charged, indicted, or convicted of crimes such as murder.

VI. *"You shall not commit adultery."*

Sufferers of Scrup/OCD are again reminded that thoughts are not actions.

VII. *"You shall not steal."*

Survey results resoundingly suggest that people with Scrup/OCD keep this commandment. Reports from respondents document their concern not to steal, embezzle, or defraud others.

VIII. *"You shall not bear false witness against your neighbor."*

To say that someone is "scrupulously honest" is to pay them a high compliment. Perhaps people with Scrup/OCD will recognize this and offer themselves affirmation.

IX. *"You shall not covet your neighbor's wife."*

This commandment is similar to the sixth commandment. Scrupulous people need reminding that thoughts are not deeds.

X. *"You shall not covet your neighbor's goods."*

The catechism notes that the spirit of this commandment forbids greed and avarice. A number of scrupulous people in the survey wondered about the gravity of their envious thoughts. Competition and materialism have been with us always. Conflicts over industry, land, international boundaries, religious dogma, and cultural pride have led to wars killing hundreds of millions of people. Perhaps the rest of the world can learn from people with scrupulosity concerning this commandment.

Chapter 14

THE LILIES OF THE FIELD

In this chapter I hope to summarize the major findings of this book and then provide my own opinions and observations. We need to break from the doctrinaire writings on OCD to look at this disorder in more creative ways.

Historical and Professional Findings

In the past five centuries religious writers have viewed scrupulosity as a difficult malady to treat. This pessimism continued until the past decade when mental health professionals began to find some success in treating OCD.

It was found, first, that certain medications can have a dramatic effect on a small number of individuals with Scrup/OCD. With many other individuals, drugs provided moderate benefits. Again I cite Edna Foa, world renowned researcher on OCD, who estimated that medication helps about "40 percent of people with OCD to improve their symptoms about 40 percent."

Second, behavior therapy helps in eliminating specific compulsive behaviors. Again, Foa provides these statistics: "in the long term, about 75–80 percent of the people are helped" (Interview with Dr. Edna Foa, December 13, 1995).

According to these figures, therefore, behavior therapy doesn't help a significant percentage of people with OCD. Using Foa's data, and the commonly established incidence rate of OCD as 2 percent of the population, and a U.S. population of approximately 250 million, it would appear that up to three million of the five million OCD sufferers would not benefit by medication. As for behavior therapy, it would appear that up to one million sufferers (20 percent) would not obtain long-term benefits. I think we can do better, and I'm not sure that greater sophistication in medications or behavior therapy is the answer.

Third, on the basis of our study of over one thousand individuals, scrupulosity appears intertwined with obsessive compulsive disorder. It is a unique manifestation, yet one with different implications.

Other empirical findings from our survey include the following. Scrup/OCD affects a wide range of people in widely different manners. Despite the lessening of this syndrome since Vatican II, Scrup/OCD continues to have a significant impact on many Catholics and others as well. Moral scrupulosity may be more prevalent in society as a whole than ever imagined. Among survey respondents, many tried treating their condition through the sacrament of confession with poor results. Of subjects evaluated in 1989, 78 percent rated medication as helping them to some degree.

Among this group, about the same percentage said that psychological therapy was similarly helpful. Especially interesting was that 85 percent of persons who had tried spiritual direction rated it helpful. This is a highly personal, often directive, empathetic relationship between minister and believer.

This study described the waxing and waning of scrupulosity in the lifetimes of many persons. We have described how this has affected their work, romantic lives, marriages, families, and involvement with friends. Consistent with findings on obsessive compulsive disorder in general, 64 percent of sufferers with Scrup/OCD also acknowledged a notable level of depression.

A follow-up survey on medications in 1995 yielded some surprising results. Consistent with estimates of the effects of medication provided by pharmaceutical companies and psychiatric researchers, a small number of people reported truly outstanding gains due to medication. However, for many people medication was no panacea.[44]

My Own Observations

I was inspired by reading the one thousand survey responses sent to me by members of Scrupulous Anonymous. I was struck by the number of people who wrote with admiration and gratitude directed toward specific physicians, therapists, or clergy who helped them with their Scrup/OCD. Effective traits of these helpers were immense compassion and empathy, availability between meetings, a strong, authoritarian presence when needed, and a willingness and ability to delve into other problems — past or present. Scrup/OCD defenses may hide these other problems from sufferers and therapists alike. I think that one part of the effectiveness of behavior therapy and even the prescription of medication is the presence of hope in the helper. Unfortunately, the studies on OCD that I have reviewed don't appear to examine this factor in detail.

In my own professional life I have worked with many therapists or reviewed their work, and I have seen psychoanalytic therapists fail. Their lack of competence or their unique interpretation of theories often contributed to their lack of success in treating OCD. I have also been impressed by master therapists.[45]

I have experienced frustration and disappointment because of the seeming lack of coordination between talk therapists, behavior therapists, and medical doctors. Because of this, we professionals aren't doing the best that we are capable of.

Much more research needs to look at the characteristics of effective therapists who work with OCD. There are probably some excellent therapists "out there" who practice psychodynamic therapy or some combination of therapies whose success rate is high. It may be even higher than the success rates of advocates of behavior therapy/medication. The best help might include behavior therapy, medication, and certain qualities in the therapist like an ability to look at trauma or misperceptions from the past and an awareness of spiritual and religious dimensions. This ambitious study is within our abilities.

Some observations on the pharmaceutical industry and OCD are relevant. While researching a graduate lecture on pharmacology, I reviewed every issue of the *American Journal of Psychiatry* since 1918. In the years before 1948, physicians tried every conceivable medication and hormone to treat severe mental illness. This was an empirical approach; others would call it trial and error or hit and miss. Most concoctions didn't work. When someone noted that Thorazine quelled the hallucinations of psychotic people, modern psychiatry received a boost. Then in the early 1960s, ads for drugs started appearing in the journal. At first simple black-and-white affairs, these advertisements now are four-color multipage layouts that cost huge sums of money. Drug companies woo physicians through slick media campaigns. A review of articles in the *American Journal of Psychiatry* demonstrates the powerful effect of financial support from the drug industry.

The role of trust, and its development by talk therapies, is stressed by Steven Levenkron. Levenkron believes that a "trusting" presence of a parent or therapist can be extremely helpful for a person suffering with OCD. "For trust you need to have a relationship with another human being," Levenkron notes. "Erikson wrote about the need to develop intimacy instead of isolation. I change this to 'intimacy instead of obsessiveness.' The implication is that therapists or significant others have to be a trusting presence." Levenkron provides what he calls "a silly example from my own life." He states:

> I'm a little obsessive regarding my car: knocks, dents, scratches, etc. So the first week I had my car, I decided it was too far back in the garage and I wanted it closer to the door. So instead of opening the garage door, starting the car, and backing it up — I just released the hand brake and gave it a push.
>
> As soon as it started rolling, it couldn't stop. It was 3600 pounds after all. So it went "bang" into the hardware of the garage door. I saw a little circle on the bumper of the car, an indentation from the garage door.
>
> I was immediately filled with adrenaline and very upset. My brain chemistry had gone haywire. I walked into the kitchen and said to my wife, "I just banged up the new car!" She came out, looked at the bumper, and said, "Do you realize now that everyone who gets down on their hands and knees within three inches of this bumper will see it?" She said, "It's fine; forget it."
>
> And I transpose this example to that of therapist/patient. There needs to be someone to provide feedback in situations like the above. (Interview with Steven Levenkron)

I hope that someday someone will do a study on Scrup/OCD this way: Recruit a large group of persons willing to participate. Assign them to a *range* of treatments, including behavior therapy, medication therapy, behavior therapy plus medication therapy, talk therapy, talk therapy plus behavior therapy, talk therapy plus medication therapy, and talk therapy plus behavior therapy plus medication therapy. The research design could be magnified by including spiritual direction as another dimension. I don't think it's fair or right to discount the potentially healing role of talk therapies practiced by experienced and competent therapists until such a research design *demonstrates* that they don't work! I would be delighted if an organization such as the OCD Foundation took on such a potentially helpful endeavor and organized all sources of therapeutic help into a powerful new arsenal to combat OCD.

"Vobis Sum Episcopus, Vobiscum Christianus"

People with Scrup/OCD need the combined healing resources of their religious tradition and the approaches of modern medical and behavioral science. To obtain some assistance on this issue, I traveled to Albany, New York, to meet with Bishop Howard J. Hubbard (Interview with Bishop Howard Hubbard, December 8, 1995). We had met twelve years ago when I interviewed him for another book. Bishop Hubbard impresses me with his vision, compassion, and skill in getting to the essence of complicated problems. Among his many achievements as bishop of Albany, he has brought to the diocese St. Bernard's Institute, a richly staffed graduate school which, among its many accomplishments, links the fields of religion and psychology. As he has done on other complex and taxing contemporary problems, Bishop Hubbard offered ideas that get to the heart of Scrup/OCD issues:

> I used to see a lot more scrupulosity prior to the Second Vatican Council. As a bishop I don't celebrate the sacrament of Reconciliation that often, but when I was a parish priest in the 1960s and 1970s it was not uncommon to have people coming to confession weekly who without question were scrupulous. I found that what they needed to do was to establish a trusting relationship with the confessor. He had to assure them of their own self-worth and try to urge them to put their trust in his counsel, even if they felt they were unworthy to receive Communion or that they were not making much progress.

Very often, if they put their trust in the confessor this gave them the impetus they needed to be able to receive the sacraments and live a more tranquil life. Very often, even those who continued to be plagued by scrupulous impulses and feelings were able to function more effectively with the assurance of the confessor that they should not be so paralyzed.

In our survey many participants complained about negative church teaching. They referred to harsh interpretations of the faith in documents such as older catechism texts. I asked Bishop Hubbard if he had any thoughts about the greater focus on positive aspects of the faith, exemplified by the catechism. Bishop Hubbard stated:

I think that in the new catechism people will see that the emphasis, particularly in the sacrament of Reconciliation, is not so much the enumeration of sins and specific details, but on the person's understanding that our God is a God of love, who is anxious — who is almost overanxious, you might say, to reach out and embrace the penitent, and to forgive the sin and heal the sinner.

With the new catechism, I think there's much more emphasis on trust in God's providence and on the loving relationship between the Lord and the penitent, and not as much emphasis on the sin itself and all the attendant rituals of the sacrament of confession such as the exact number of sins and all the circumstances.

I think it's helpful for scrupulous people to understand that feelings in and of themselves are not bad, but it's what we do with them that is important. Feelings are neutral. The fact that someone has a feeling of anger or lust or discouragement — that in and of itself is part of the human condition and is morally neutral. It's only when we act on these feelings that we might be capable of improper behavior. Such an understanding could be helpful to a scrupulous penitent.

Bishop Hubbard encouraged sufferers of Scrup/OCD and pastoral workers who minister to them to take advantage of the

effective discoveries of psychiatry, behavior therapy, and psychotherapy:

> I think that drug therapies and psychotherapies that are
> available can be of great assistance to people with scrupulos-
> ity, and I would encourage people to seek them out and use
> them. Sometimes people say, "I feel guilty about using drugs;
> I should be able to do this naturally." But I think that drugs
> are part of God's creation. We should see them as a tool that
> God has given us to help us deal with certain realities of the
> human condition.
>
> I think there continues to be a certain stigma associated
> with emotional and mental problems. If you've got a pain
> in your side, if you've got an arthritic problem, you don't
> feel guilty because it's something physical. People say, "This
> is something I don't have any control over, and I'm just go-
> ing to take the medication the doctor prescribes." But when
> people say, "I've got an obsessive compulsive disorder," well,
> there's still that layover of moral impropriety that we should
> be able to control this by an act of the will.

Bishop Hubbard encouraged people suffering from scrupulosity
and obsessive compulsive disorder

> ... to understand that these emotional and psychiatric prob-
> lems can be due to a causation that is beyond one's ability
> to control by the will, but can be assisted either through
> therapy or drug treatment, or a combination of these. I
> think these therapies are not only acceptable, but are actu-
> ally something very good, and it should be seen as one of
> God's gifts to humanity that we now have resources such as
> these available.

Many readers will wonder about the Latin heading for this
section. At the risk of embarrassing Bishop Hubbard I will explain. "Vobis sum episcopus, vobiscum christianus" is a phrase
from the writings of St. Augustine, bishop of Hippo, meaning
"I am a bishop for you, I am a Christian with you" (see Pope
John Paul II, *Crossing the Threshold of Hope*, 14). As a leader
Bishop Hubbard displays abundant compassion, tremendous capacity to listen, alacrity of judgment, deep faith, and ability to be
firm and provide direction when required. His people trust him.

We, as therapists, as fellow pilgrims, and as parents might consider that these traits figure highly in the healing of Scrup/OCD and augment the behavioral and medical approaches dominating much of the professional literature.

Encouragement Beyond Therapy

Scrup/OCD vexes and exasperates professionals and family members. These people need reassurance. In reviewing the psychological and religious writings on Scrup/OCD, it appeared to me that there is a link, unrecognized by many, between the Catholic Sacrament of Anointing, psychological disorders in general, and Scrup/OCD in particular. Traditionally this Catholic sacrament had been referred to as "Extreme Unction" and was reserved for times of critical illness. However, a broadened understanding of this sacrament keeps in mind that New Testament understandings of the words "sickness" and "meek in spirit" also include psychological problems, distress, and even mental retardation. It appears that this sacrament is appropriate for sufferers of Scrup/OCD. With this in mind I asked Bishop Hubbard to review the following suggestions. These are offered to sufferers of Scrup/OCD, pastoral workers, and the psychological community.

•

ANOINTING OF THOSE WITH SCRUPULOSITY/OCD: PASTORAL GUIDELINES

The Apostolic Constitution *Sacram unctionem infirmorum* states:

> The sacrament of the Anointing of the Sick is given to those who are seriously ill by anointing them on the forehead and hands with duly blessed oil — pressed from olives or from other plants — saying only once: "Through this holy anointing may the Lord in his love and mercy help you with the grace of the Holy Spirit. May the Lord who frees you from sin save you and raise you up." (Pope Paul VI, *Sacram unctionem infirmorum*, November 30, 1972)

Modern medical science documents the severe and debilitating effects of scrupulosity and obsessive compulsive disorder. This condition causes sorrow, depression, and hopelessness. Scrupulosity can become a trap — a force that seizes — and can keep a person from regular reception of the sacraments of Penance and the Eucharist.

In cases of severe scrupulosity and obsessive compulsive disorder, the sacrament of the Anointing of the Sick could be considered. This would not be administered in place of psychological or medical help but would rather serve as encouragement to these persons to become united regularly with Christ in the sacraments of Reconciliation and Holy Communion.

Some thoughts to be considered prior to the Anointing:

- Psychological illness can cause severe suffering, trauma that may be hidden from others.

- Despite efforts of tremendous will power by the sufferer, scrupulosity and obsessive compulsive disorder can cause one to be alienated from others at home, in the community, in the church, and from Our Lord.

- This Anointing is not to be considered in a magical way that would set up false expectations but is rather an acknowledgment by the church of the debilitating effects of a severe psychological illness. Moreover, it is an invitation to proceed to regular reception of the other sacraments.

- Persons with this disorder are encouraged to seek out the fullness of professional assistance available.

The following might be considered for inclusion in a preparatory prayer:

Lord, your Apostle James wrote that "anyone among you who is ill should send for the elders of the church, and they must anoint the sick person with oil in the name of the Lord, and pray over him."

Psychological distress can be a time of trouble and trial, lasting months, years, and even decades. Persons in such agony often remain isolated and their suffering unknown. May this sacrament be a way of reaching out and recognizing this distress.

In the church there is a long history of persons who have suffered from scrupulosity. The burdens of St. Veronica Guliani, St. Ignatius,

*and St. Alphonsus are well known. May the lives of saints like
these remind us that there is always hope. May the healing approaches of therapy and modern medical science provide further
encouragement for this person.*

Dear Father, as you helped Jesus endure his final peirasmous *—
that troubled, agonizing, and anguishing time between Gethsemane
and Calvary — please give this person your extra help and grace.*[46]
*Please inspire his/her doctor or therapist to be an instrument of
your healing.*

*Let this Anointing be an invitation to Reconciliation and Eu-
charist: to approach these great avenues of healing and nourishment
in a human rather than "perfect" way.*

*Unite this person once again with his/her brothers and sisters,
parents, children, and friends in your church. Remind him/her that
no one is without a family in this world: the church is a home
and family for everyone, especially those who "labor and are heavy
laden."*

Following such preparatory prayers the actual words and actions of the
Anointing, as noted above and in Paul VI, apostolic constitution *Sacram
unctionem infirmorum,* November 30, 1972, may be provided.

•

Bishop Hubbard commented on this use of the sacrament of the
Anointing of the Sick:

As I read this, I think it's very much on target. I know
that the same idea comes up sometimes, analogously you
might say, with addictions such as alcohol and drugs. I
know that many feel that these conditions are severe life-
threatening illnesses, involving lifelong recovery, and that a
person who has illnesses such as these can avail themselves
of the sacrament of the sick.

I think also that scrupulosity and obsessive compulsive
disorder is an illness that causes severe psychic and emotional trauma to the individual — severe pain that can be
even more traumatizing than physical pain. I do think that
persons who have this disorder can avail themselves of this

spiritual resource for emotional and spiritual healing. I can say that this is well within the bounds of who is eligible to celebrate the sacrament of the sick.

I conclude quoting Bishop Hubbard's encouragement to people with Scrup/OCD:

One of my favorite passages in the scriptures is the famous one about the lilies of the field.

> "That is why I am telling you not to worry about your life and what you are to eat, nor about your body and what you are to wear. Surely life is more than food, and the body more than clothing! Look at the birds in the sky. They do not sow or reap or gather into barns; yet your heavenly Father feeds them. Are you not worth much more than they are? Can any of you, however much you worry, add one single cubit to your span of life? And why worry about clothing? Think of the flowers growing in the fields; they never have to work or spin; yet I assure you that not even Solomon in all his royal robes was clothed like one of these. Now if that is how God clothes the wild flowers growing in the field which are there today and thrown into the furnace tomorrow, will he not much more look after you, you who have so little faith?
>
> "So do not worry; do not say, 'What are we to eat? What are we to drink? What are we to wear?' Your Heavenly Father knows you need them all. So set your hearts on his kingdom first, and on God's saving justice, and all these other things will be given you as well. So do not worry about tomorrow: tomorrow will take care of itself. Each day has enough trouble of its own."

I think this whole idea of trust in God's providence, which historically has meant for scrupulous people to put their trust in a confessor, now includes trusting an authority figure such as a physician or therapist. And this is fine, but we can also remember that there's no greater authority figure, no greater lover, and no greater forgiver than God. We can put our trust in God's providence, and put our scruples and put our obsessions or compulsions in the Lord's hands, and say, "Lord, I don't know what to do with these, but I trust in your Providence. You know what's in the bottom of my heart, and I leave it to you. I put it in your heart and ask you to help take these compulsions away." (Interview with Bishop Howard Hubbard, December 8, 1995)

Chapter 15

I LIFT UP MY EYES
TO THE MOUNTAIN

"Scrupulosity," wrote Joseph Cardinal Bernardin, "is a great inner suffering for so many."

For over forty years Cardinal Bernardin worked indefatigably as priest, bishop, archbishop, and cardinal, and in the months preceding his death of cancer he found time to review this book and to offer encouragement to those who would be reading it.

"Why not consider including in the text some of the Psalms — prayers inspired by God — in more than one place in the book," he suggested. "Some of the Psalms are very comforting. I would suggest, for example: Psalm 8, Psalm 23, Psalm 63:1–9, and Psalm 121" (personal correspondence with Joseph Cardinal Bernardin, November 1, 1995, and April 3, 1996). In preceding chapters readers have been alerted to places in the text where material from these verses is pertinent.

These Psalms are presented so that readers, whether those who experience scrupulosity themselves or those who help them, can strive for the peacefulness offered by the spirit of the Psalmist and the life of the cardinal:

Psalm 8: O Lord, our Lord, How glorious is your name over all the earth.

O Lord, our Lord,
    how awesome is your name through all the earth!
    You have set your majesty above the heavens!
Out of the mouths of babes and infants
    you have drawn a defense against your foes,
    to silence enemy and avenger.

When I see your heavens, the work of your fingers,
  the moon and the stars that you set in place —
What are humans that you are mindful of them,
  mere mortals that you care for them?
Yet you have made them little less than a god,
  crowned with glory and honor.
You have given them rule over the works of your hands,
  put all things at their feet:
All sheep and oxen,
  even the beasts of the field,
The birds of the air, the fish of the sea,
  and whatever swims the paths of the seas.
O LORD, our Lord,
  how awesome is your name through all the earth!

Psalm 23: The Lord is my Shepherd

The LORD is my shepherd;
  there is nothing I lack.
in green pastures you let me graze;
  to safe waters you lead me;
  you restore my strength.
You guide me along the right path
  for the sake of your name.
Even when I walk through a dark valley,
  I fear no harm for you are at my side;
  your rod and staff give me courage.
You set a table before me
  as my enemies watch;
You anoint my head with oil;
  my cup overflows.
Only goodness and love will pursue me
  all the days of my life;
I will dwell in the house of the LORD
  for years to come.

Psalm 63: O God, you are my God whom I seek

O God, you are my God —
  for you I long!

For you my body yearns;
   for you my soul thirsts,
Like a land parched lifeless,
   and without water.
So I look to you in the sanctuary
   to see your power and glory.
For your love is better than life;
   my lips offer your worship.
I will bless you as long as I live;
   I will lift up my hands, calling on your name.
My soul shall savor the rich banquet of praise,
   with joyous lips my mouth shall honor you!
When I think of you upon my bed,
   through the night watches I will recall
That you indeed are my help,
   and in the shadow of your wings I shout for you.

Psalm 121: I lift up my eyes to the mountain

I raise my eyes toward the mountains.
   From where will my help come?
My help comes from the LORD,
   the maker of heaven and earth.
God will not allow your foot to slip;
   your guardian does not sleep.
Truly, the guardian of Israel
   never slumbers or sleeps.
The LORD is your guardian;
   the LORD is your shade
   at your right hand.
By day the sun cannot harm you,
   nor the moon by night.
The LORD will guard you from all evil,
   will always guard your life.
The LORD will guard your coming and going
   both now and forever.

Appendix

SURVEY RESULTS

The following is a presentation of the statistical data from our survey of the members of Scrupulous Anonymous, presented at three conventions of the American Psychological Association. Some things need to be said regarding this data and to what degree it represents scrupulous people in general. As studies in psychology go, it is a very large sample. Over eight thousand questionnaires were mailed to members, and over one thousand were returned.

Some limitations of this survey are to be noted, but an understanding of these can help in further investigations of scrupulosity. People in this group identified themselves as being scrupulous. They may also have had other conditions present that have not been adequately classified. Many members of this group were above the age of forty-five. This is the approximate age of people who would have received religious education in the "pre–Vatican II" days. Many of these have been noted in the text. There were, however, many respondents below the age of forty-five who still suffer from scrupulosity.

This group is primarily Roman Catholic. The literature suggests that scrupulosity is most common in the Catholic Church and in Orthodox branches of Judaism. However, it would be interesting to do an extended survey of this question.

A presentation and discussion of the data follows. All figures represent percentages.

Demographic Characteristics of the Sample

Sex

Female	68
Male	32

Age

21–45	26.6
46–69	54.7
70–99	19.7

The mean age for the sample was 56.4 years old. It is assumed that most of the 26.6 percent of the sample below the age of forty-five would not have experienced significant training in the pre–Vatican II Church. Those over the age of forty-five would most certainly have been trained in the more traditional emphasis on rules and regulations that characterized the pre–Vatican II Church.

Occupation

Homemaker	22.1
Retired	22.1
Laborer	15.1
Teacher/educator	12.8
Clerical worker	11.6
Sales	7.0
Nurse	3.5
Counselor	1.6
M.D.	1.6
Public service worker	1.2
Librarian	.4
Priest/nun	.4
Unemployed	.4

It is interesting that highly educated persons such as physicians are represented in the sample. It is also interesting that only .4 percent of the sample are unemployed — significantly below the national average.

Marital Status

Single	24.7
Married	57.0
Divorced	6.4
Other	11.2

Education

Less than high school	5.0
High school	45.4
College	29.0
Professional	20.6

Type of Home Environment

Single parent	2.6
Caring parent	9.3
Strict parents	14.8
Abusive environment	5.9
Large family	17.0
Small family	11.9
Religious environment	8.1
Alcoholic parent	5.9

Current Religious Practices

Daily Communion	32.2
Daily rosary	48.5
Weekly Mass	64.8
No weekly Mass	32.6
Weekly Communion	50.0
Read "Office"	10.6

While many attend daily Mass, say the rosary, or read the Office, a substantial number do not go to weekly Mass and a substantial number do not go to weekly Communion. It has been noted that Communion is a problematic area for scrupulous people, for many reasons, and the data appear to support this.

Religious Practices of Birth Family

Very religious	17.8
Practicing	65.5
Separate religions	5.6
Not religious	10.2

It is surprising that a great many people came from backgrounds that were not described as extremely religious. This suggests factors in the development of scrupulosity other than an extremely religious family.

Religious Practices of Current Family

Very religious	17.3
Practicing	77.7
Separate	1.5
Not religious	1.9

The majority of respondents are practicing Catholics, at a level above the national norm.

Do You Consider Yourself a Religious Person?

No	10.1
Yes	89.9

Have You Tried to Treat Your Scrupulosity through Confession?

Yes	71.8
No	28.2

Many respondents acknowledged that confession could be very difficult for them because it stirred up more anxieties, and some respondents avoided confession altogether. Although Catholics in general are going to this sacrament in fewer numbers, it is thought that the avoidance by 28 percent in this sample is due more to their scrupulosity; they think they should go — but don't — and then feel guilty.

Have You Been in Therapy?

Yes   35.0
No   65.0

The low percentage of people who have been in therapy is surprising. It suggests that many scrupulous people in this sample have not taken advantage of all the help available. Many respondents noted bad experiences with therapists, particularly therapists who lumped all religious practices together as signs of guilt or other problems. A scrupulous person requires a therapist who is sensitive to the positive aspects of religious experience in order to encourage the practices to replace scrupulous ones.

Medication

No   66.2
Yes   33.8

That one of three respondents has tried medication affirms the painful nature of scrupulosity.

Spiritual Direction

Yes   61.3
No   38.7

Spiritual direction is one of the most frequently sought forms of help. It would be interesting to survey the spiritual directors themselves concerning the manner in which spiritual direction occurs and how effective they perceive it to be. Note that nearly twice as many people in the sample had tried spiritual direction as had tried medication.

Reading Books/Bibliotherapy

Yes   78.6
No   20.7

Reading books is the most frequent way that scrupulous people try to make themselves feel better. One goal of this book is to make scrupulous readers aware of books that have been written specifically on OCD so that they can avail themselves of the latest learnings from psychology.

EFFECTIVENESS OF VARIOUS TREATMENTS

Confession

Made it worse	13.7
A little worse	4.7
No change	7.7
Helped some	30.8
Helped a great deal	39.3
Cured	2.6

Two interesting findings emerge. First is the number of people who report that confession helped them "a great deal." Second, over 26 percent of respondents found that confession did not help or made their condition worse.

Spiritual Direction

Made it worse	2.6
A little worse	1.0
No change	8.7
Helped some	31.8
Helped a great deal	50.3
Cured	4.6

Spiritual direction received high endorsement from respondents. In addition to the spiritual direction, the empathy and accepting nature of the spiritual director were no doubt factors here.

Therapy

Made it worse	2.5
A little worse	10.6
No change	7.4
Helped some	42.6
Helped a great deal	33.6
Cured	3.3

The helpfulness of psychological therapy is affirmed by participants.

Medication

Made it worse	5.3
A little worse	1.1
No change	13.7
Helped some	35.8
Helped a great deal	42.1
Cured	2.0

Medication is also considered very helpful. This high rating was given by participants in 1989, when Anafranil had not been approved for use in the United States and Prozac was just starting to be used. Since that time, these two medications have been used extensively for OCD, with effectiveness. The medications are believed to effect the reuptake of Serotonin, a brain neurotransmitter. In addition, there are new SRIs (Serotonin Reuptake Inhibitors) such as Zoloft and Paxil, which have also been prescribed for OCD.

Most respondents reported that the symptoms of their scrupulosity waxed and waned over the course of their life. This parallels the description of OCD in the professional literature. First, respondents were asked to rate the interference of scrupulosity in their life when it was at its mildest.

AT ITS BEST, HOW DID YOUR SCRUPULOSITY INTERFERE WITH...?

Friends

Very severe	4.3
Severe	11.5
Somewhat	35.5
Very little	48.3

Friendship, a healing balm for sufferers of any physical or emotional problems, was negatively affected by scrupulosity for over half of the respondents, and this was when their reported scrupulosity was at its "best."

Romance

Very severe	12.6
Severe	17.8
Somewhat	36.4
Very little	32.2

The majority of respondents indicated that scrupulosity affected their romantic life. One concern of many respondents was whether to tell prospective marital partners of their scrupulosity.

Marriage

Very severe	11.7
Severe	19.9
Somewhat	36.2
Very little	31.6

Marriage is difficult without scrupulosity or OCD, and respondents suggest that their scrupulosity adds to marital strife even when their symptoms are at a minimal level.

School

Very severe	5.5
Severe	12.9
Somewhat	32.8
Very little	48.3

Research on OCD has found that, in general, personal relationships are affected more than school or occupational performance. The results of our survey are consistent with this finding. However, a significant number, almost 20 percent, concede that at its best scrupulosity still had a severe or very severe effect on their school functioning.

Work

Very severe	5.2
Severe	17.3
Somewhat	44.6
Very little	32.9

Again, the effect on work is less than on relationships.

AT ITS WORST, HOW DID SCRUPULOSITY INTERFERE WITH...?

Friends

Very severe	14.9
Severe	17.2
Somewhat	33.5
Very little	34.4

Romance

Very severe	27.7
Severe	22.3
Somewhat	27.2
Very little	22.3

Marriage

Very severe	24.6
Severe	28.3
Somewhat	24.1
Very little	23.0

School

Very severe	19.1
Severe	14.4
Somewhat	31.9
Very little	34.0

Work

Very severe	16.8
Severe	27.9
Somewhat	30.5
Very little	24.8

Having Children?

No	70.7
Yes	15.2

The figure regarding interference with having children may be higher than what sufferers of OCD might report, due to traditional Catholic teachings on the importance of children. The suffering of the group who reported interference should not be underestimated. There have been some moving personal stories in the OCD Foundation newsletter concerning the effect of OCD on motherhood.

Has Scrupulosity Affected Any Other Family Members?

None	53.7
Mother	25.0
Sister	3.7
Brother	2.7
Father	12.2
Spouse	1.1
Other member	1.6

Over 37 percent of respondents noted that one of their parents had scrupulosity also. Whether scrupulosity is learned or inherited is still unknown. There are few respondents with a scrupulous spouse. Scrupulous people tend not to marry each other.

Has Scrupulosity Appeared and Disappeared over Your Lifetime?

Yes	66.1
No	31.1

Has Scrupulosity Gotten Better or Worse during Your Lifetime?

Yes	85.5
No	11.6

This data suggests the recurring and changing nature of scrupulosity.

Check Three Adjectives That Your Friends
Would Use to Describe You

Devoted worker	50.7
Hardworking	55.2
Successful	17.0
Reserved	35.6
Uncreative	4.4
Apprehensive	24.4
Assertive	9.6
Tense	35.8
Practical	28.5
Emotional	27.3
Expedient	1.9
Venturesome	4.6

Sports and Exercise You Participate in Weekly

Walking	63.5
Cycling	10.0
Jogging	8.0
Aerobics	7.2
Nautilus	3.2
Swimming	7.2
Other	23.3

Walking and cycling appear to be the favored means of exercise for this group.

Health Problems Experienced

High blood pressure	31.4
Severe headache	27.0
Heart attack	6.3
Asthma	8.1
Diabetes	3.8
Overweight	41.0
Depression	64.0
Workaholism	25.0
Drinking too much	11.4
Anorexia	4.2
Perfectionism	66.0

Three findings are significant. First, 64 percent report the presence of depression. This is consistent with reports regarding OCD in general. Does the scrupulosity cause the depression by keeping the person alienated from healthy and rewarding religious and interpersonal pursuits? Another noteworthy finding is that 11.4 percent report that they drink too much. This is significant because therapists need to address this issue — often before they help the person deal with the scrupulosity. Third is the finding that 66 percent consider themselves to be perfectionists.

Are There Possessions That You Collect?

None	42.2
Statues	3.2
Coins	2.7
Junk	2.2
Money, savings	8.6
Clothes	4.3
Books, magazines	21.6
Household items	1.6
Written letters	4.3
Religious objects	2.2
Other	7.0

Writers on OCD have suggested a "Pack Rat" connection: the tendency of sufferers of OCD to collect things. Over half the respondents acknowledged that they "collect things."

How Has Scrupulosity Helped in Your Life?

No help	28.9
More honest	7.6
More serious	2.0
Greater belief in God	21.6
More sympathetic, empathic	11.3
More moral	18.1

Despite the suffering, many respondents are able to find something helpful in being scrupulous.

NOTES

1. I have been unable to find statistics on the prevalence of scrupulosity in other religions. It would be interesting to obtain data for different Protestant groups, particularly fundamentalist sects, as well as for people of the Jewish faith. Another religion which may encourage scrupulous tendencies is the Muslim faith. Muslim practices include washing as a means of purification prior to eating.

2. Some biological researchers hypothesize that obsessive compulsive disorder may be triggered in "primitive" regions of the brain, namely, those that developed before the cerebral cortex. Ethologists hypothesize that routinized stereotypical behaviors by animals such as birds and fishes are similar to obsessive compulsive mechanisms in human beings. The development of PET (positron emission tomography) scans and the ability to measure ongoing neurochemical activity may produce interesting results in years to come.

3. In October 1989 we sent ten thousand four-page questionnaires to all members of Scrupulous Anonymous. We received responses from every state in the U.S.A., Canada, Europe, South America, Asia, and Australia. Qualitative review of responses suggests that scrupulosity is universal.

4. There appears to be some misinformation among current OCD researchers concerning historical descriptions of obsessive compulsive disorder. For example, S. Rauch and M. Jenike in their article "Neuro-biological Models of Obsessive Compulsive Disorder" assert: "In the middle ages, symptoms suggestive of OCD were attributed to demonic possession and treated by exorcism. Not until the beginning of the twentieth century had the disorder been described formally and psychological theories developed" (20). As we shall see throughout this book there have been extensive and eloquent phenomenologies of scrupulosity/obsessive compulsive disorder going back centuries. In addition, there are treatment approaches, ideas still relevant today, which in combination with current psychological and medical approaches augment and enhance the total treatment.

5. Augustinus Gemelli wrote the theoretical and empirical book *De Scrupulis: Psychopathologiae Specimen in Usum Confessariorum.* I am indebted to Marc vanderHeyden for his skillful and eloquent assistance in translating Gemelli. Any errors of interpretation are solely my responsibility.

6. I hope that this book encourages greater discussion among those who study OCD and Scrup/OCD. Perhaps it can serve as a "Vatican II" among researchers.

7. Freud's eloquent description of OCD symptoms, and in particular the awful torment evoked by mental obsessions, is worth while reading for thera-

pists of any theoretical model. Whether you agree with Freud's treatments or not, Freud, like Linnaeus in biology, offers superb scientific descriptions.

8. It is interesting that Gemelli hypothesized about the relationship between mental tics and obsessive compulsive disorder in 1914.

9. I think scrupulosity is worthy of inclusion as a separate form of OCD. I hope it will be considered for the next revision of DSM IV or for the new edition of DSM V.

10. Just as one swallow doesn't make a summer, some symptoms of OCD don't imply the full-blown psychiatric disorder.

11. Judith Rapoport acknowledges scrupulosity in her book *The Boy Who Couldn't Stop Washing* (1990).

12. These are expressed masterfully by Father Vincent O'Flaherty in his 1966 book *How to Cure Scruples*.

13. This research (Van Ornum, Askin, Paultre, and White 1990) was presented at the 98th annual convention of the American Psychological Association, Boston, Massachusetts, August 21, 1990.

14. As with problems with alcohol and substance abuse, it is important that family members not enable OCD behaviors and hence unwittingly magnify the power of OCD. See Livingston 1989.

15. A number of articles from the past fifteen years in the *American Journal of Psychiatry* have defined and explored alexithymia. For example, see Ahrens and Deffner 1986, 430–47. I think that further empirical study of Scrup/OCD could include alexithymia as a dimension or research variable.

16. It is always important for therapists to inquire about drug and alcohol use among persons with any anxiety disorder.

17. Freud wrote about the reification of language in people with OCD. People with OCD equate thinking with doing. Even the most fleeting and transient thought is transformed into an act. This may help explain the tendency of many Catholics with Scrup/OCD to genuinely believe that fleeting thoughts of an aggressive or sexual nature signify a mortal sin.

18. This surprisingly liberal and psychologically sophisticated statement on masturbation in a document approved by Pope John Paul II may provide comfort to sufferers of Scrup/OCD and may surprise therapists or others who view the church as being burdened with an antiquated and medieval sense of sexuality. The citation is from the *Catechism of the Catholic Church*, no. 2352.

19. Numerous articles in the professional literature suggest the co-existence of OCD and depression.

20. I am grateful to Dr. George Mora, the medical director at the Astor Home for Children for over twenty-five years and an eminent psychiatric historian. Dr. Mora advised me that Father Gemelli had written a book on scrupulosity. A survey of libraries in North America indicated that there were several copies of this book in Latin and several copies in a German translation which was published at the beginning of World War I. There may have been an original edition of this book in Italian, but it does not seem to be available on the North American continent. The appearance of this book in three languages during a decade of psychiatric and global upheaval suggests the importance of scrupulosity among early twentieth-century mental health professionals.

21. I am grateful to Joseph Campo for providing me with further information on Augustinus Gemelli.

22. Although many mental health professionals acknowledge William James and his sensitivity toward religious experience, I think it would be very helpful for mental health professionals to link the ideas of William James to empirical studies involving religion and mental health. Professional or academic readers may be interested in related articles in the *Journal for the Scientific Study of Religion*. Psychologists might benefit from the work of division 36 of the American Psychological Association, Psychologists Interested in Religion.

23. It may be that the constant ruminating and obsessing which accompany scrupulosity may engender creative thinking in some individuals.

24. This book, readily available in a paperback edition from Doubleday Image Books, should be of interest to anyone who wishes to learn more about St. Ignatius or scrupulosity. It provides therapists with an excellent exposition of the cultural Catholic background that is part of Catholic scrupulosity.

25. Even modern behavioral therapists have used the concept of the devil as a metaphor to encourage sufferers of OCD to see OCD as something they are not responsible for.

26. Joseph Ciarrocchi (1995) has devised a "reporter" strategy to help scrupulous people assess the extent of scruples. I highly recommend Ciarrocchi's book.

27. Detailed accounts of the James-Lange theory can be found in any introductory psychology textbook.

28. I am grateful to Steven Levenkron for bringing to my attention *Holy Anorexia* (Bell 1985).

29. It is my impression that many if not most studies on OCD in the professional literature are comprised of subjects who enter treatment at a clinic or research hospital. This could suggest a high level of disturbance and it could also suggest that previous encounters with therapists or physicians have left their OCD symptoms undiminished. The positive side of such a phenomenon, which remains only a conjecture on my part, is that there exist in the general population successful people with OCD who either have not sought treatment or who have been in treatment and have been helped significantly, thereby making them unavailable to the current research studies being conducted.

30. I think it would be helpful for researchers to develop questionnaires or tests that would measure OCD and scrupulosity on a continuum of numerical scores.

31. It is possible that this figure underestimates the prevalence of alcohol problems within the families of our sample group. People filling out the questionnaire may have glossed over, minimized, or otherwise overlooked significant drinking problems. This is one difficulty in using a self-report questionnaire.

32. In my opinion, expert talk therapies may provide an opportunity to desensitize individuals with Scrup/OCD from troubling thoughts.

33. Foa and Wilson (1990) provide an excellent discussion on this important issue.

34. See the Annotated Bibliography for a description of *Feeling Good* by David Burns, M.D. I think this book can help people with Scrup/OCD.

35. Obsessive compulsive behaviors accompany organically based conditions such as dementia, autism, Parkinson's, severe mental retardation, as well as medical conditions related to high fevers. Despite the presence of OCD-like behaviors, the full diagnosis of obsessive compulsive disorder is usually not made in these cases. Perhaps the advent of new neuroimaging diagnostic procedures will facilitate the identification of specific cortical and sub-cortical regions that may be associated with these behaviors. I find it interesting that Gemelli also considered such linkages, but he lacked the sophisticated tools of modern neuroscience.

36. At least 95 percent of the material in the OCD newsletter, in my estimate, emphasizes these two approaches.

37. I hope that exposition of the statistics in this manner will encourage further discussion in evaluating the current as well as the potential efficacy of behavioral and medication approaches.

38. Leon Salzman is an eminent psychoanalyst who was past president of the American Psychoanalytic Association. His book *Treatment of Obsessive and Compulsive Behaviors* was first published in 1968 and has been re-released in 1994 with a new introduction.

39. One of the best books concerning psychoanalytic treatment of obsessive compulsive disorder is Leon Salzman, *The Treatment of Obsessive Compulsive Disorders*, 1994.

40. For a discussion on Aquinas and free will, see Adler 1966.

41. Jim Broatch, executive director of the OCD Foundation, has written an excellent article, "Eenie-Meenie-Miney-Moe, Catch a Doctor by His/Her Toe. If the Doctor Hollers Let Him/Her Go; Or How to Choose the Right Practitioner and Begin to Get Well," *OCD Newsletter*, 5–11.

42. The technical term "transference" denotes feelings that a patient brings in from his or her past history and "transfers" to the therapist. Presumably the therapist is a neutral stimulus and has not encouraged these feelings. An example of transference is a patient who is constantly angry at a therapist despite the therapist's competence and good clinical work. In this case, the therapist will look for life experiences in the patient that have caused the original intensity of this anger and rage. One probably has to be a master therapist to be able to do this well, since no therapist is actually a neutral stimulus. Many of the things therapists do can evoke strong feelings in clients and it is a grave error on the therapist's part—a mistake that may cause the patient to leave therapy—to attribute these feelings to the patient's background rather than what is happening in therapy itself.

There is a double dimension of transference when working with people with Scrup/OCD. Personal reactions to their life history may be transferred not only to the therapist but also to important aspects of their religion. While I don't think this approach is going to cure crippling rituals, I think it may be an important tactic after OCD rituals have been brought under control through behavior therapy and medication. Steven Levenkron devotes a great deal of case material to this concept.

43. Some interesting comments regarding scrupulosity were made by O. Hobart Mowrer in his chapter "Neurosis and Psychotherapy" included in the

volume *Psychotherapy Research and Practice,* 1949. Mowrer suggests that scrupulous people need to be aware of their moral standards and hold themselves accountable.

44. I am not confident about the external validity of the second study. In 1989 over one thousand individuals participated; the second study yielded less than one hundred. I think there is a great need for a well-designed study that would assign people with Scrup/OCD to different treatment conditions including medication prior to taking the medication.

45. Another study that I would like to see done perhaps in a journal such as *Psychological Bulletin* would be to look at the number of years of experience of the therapists treating the OCD and their competence. It is possible that the competence and experience of the therapist may be a more significant variable than theoretical models of OCD.

46. For a beautiful discussion of the phenomenology of Peirasmous, see Brown 1994.

ANNOTATED BIBLIOGRAPHY

The following list represents a wide range of therapies and religious resources. This assortment highlights a theme of this book: a creative combination of approaches is needed to battle scrupulosity/obsessive compulsive disorder. I hope that this collection will generate an ecumenical movement of sorts among sufferers of Scrup/OCD and their helpers. Perhaps advocates of certain psychological approaches will expand their consciousness of other ideas. I hope all helpers may consider becoming more familiar with religious issues that accompany scrupulosity, but most importantly that they learn about the healthy and vital religious traditions, of which scrupulosity is but a caricature and shadow. Finally, I hope that all pastoral workers will not be intimidated by psychological resources but will consider them a key part of their pastoral training.

Abata, R. 1976. *Helps for the Scrupulous.* Liguori, Mo.: Liguori Publications. This best-selling book from a major Catholic publishing house has become a classic over the past two decades. Father Abata provides a compassionate and empathic description of scrupulosity. He discusses specific issues which may be difficult for scrupulous people, such as income taxes, sexuality, and determining sin and guilt. There is a continual theme that one must "go against" scrupulous impulses, pastoral advice that is consistent with modern behavioral therapies that have been shown to be helpful. Father Abata has a doctorate in moral theology from the Angelicum University in Rome and has worked extensively with persons with scrupulosity. Father Abata belongs to the Redemptorists, the order of priests founded by St. Alphonsus Liguori.

Anxiety Disorders Center. 1989. *Obsessive Compulsive Disorder: A Guide.* Madison: University of Wisconsin. This succinct forty-four-page pamphlet is published by one of the university centers that has done a great deal of research on OCD over the years. The information contained on psychopharmacology is very valuable. This center should be a helpful resource in years ahead as new medications are developed and long-term effects of current medications are monitored.

———. 1993. *Obsessive Compulsive Disorder in Children: A Guide.* Madison: University of Wisconsin. Another succinct and highly practical guide from the University of Wisconsin, this one specializing in OCD and children. It has features similar to those of the guide listed above.

Burns, D. 1992. *Feeling Good.* New York: Avon. A book on "the new mood therapy" with numerous practical exercises that alleviate or inoculate against depression.

Catechism of the Catholic Church. 1994. New York: Image Books. This reader-friendly mass market paperback offers a clear and positive exposition of nearly three thousand key points of the Roman Catholic faith. Many readers with Scrup/OCD will find that it will help them develop a religious outlook of greater trust and maturity. Mental health professionals who are not familiar with the Roman Catholic faith will find this to be an excellent presentation of Catholic belief and culture.

Ciarrocchi, J. W. 1995. *The Doubting Disease.* New York: Paulist Press. Dr. Ciarrocchi is a clinical psychologist with extensive pastoral training. He presents an excellent overview of scrupulosity and offers a systematic and comprehensive cognitive behavioral approach to managing and controlling religious obsessions and compulsions. Similar in theme and format to Foa and Wilson's *Stop Obsessing,* this carefully produced and helpful resource will benefit both sufferers of Scrup/OCD and their helpers. By highlighting a cognitive behavioral approach Ciarrocchi's book complements the wider focus of the present volume.

Foa, E., and R. Wilson. 1991. *Stop Obsessing: How to Overcome Your Obsessions and Compulsions.* New York: Bantam Books. Dr. Edna Foa, whose helpful insights are discussed in this book, teams up with Dr. Reid Wilson in what is probably the most thorough and helpful book on the behavioral treatment of obsessive compulsive disorder. Features include questionnaires to help sufferers analyze the severity of obsessions and compulsions and a self-help program to overcome mild symptoms and reduce severe ones.

Foster, C. 1993. *Funny, You Don't Look Crazy: Life with Obsessive Compulsive Disorder.* Ellsworth, Mass.: The Ellsworth American. This remarkable book provides inspirational first-hand accounts from OCD sufferers. "Catherine's Story" (86–88) details a crippling case of religious scrupulosity which ends on a happy and hopeful note.

Freud, S. 1963. *Three Case Histories: The Wolf Man, The Rat Man, and the Psychotic Dr. Schreiber.* New York: Collier. Current thinking about OCD banishes Freud. However, a review of the reference lists of nearly every critic of Freud indicates that they have not consulted the original source — Freud himself. Such a methodology would lose points on an undergraduate term paper. Freud's understanding of the torments that bedeviled Rat Man and Wolf Man, his two cases with OCD, demonstrate great sensitivity on Freud's part. His understanding of OCD from the sufferer's point of view could be helpful to therapists or to those who prescribe medication. These cases can also be found in Freud's collected works, available in many libraries.

James, W. 1982. *The Varieties of Religious Experience: A Study in Human Nature.* New York: Penguin Books. This book is required reading for all mental health professionals who work with religious issues.

Levenkron, S. A. 1991. *Obsessive Compulsive Disorders.* New York: Warner Books. Levenkron views obsessive compulsive disorder as the personality's attempt to reduce anxieties. These may stem from painful personal experiences or a genetic tendency toward anxiety. Levenkron views the establishment and development of trust as a key issue for the person with

OCD and advocates a creative combination of talk therapy and medication. His description of how a psychopharmacologist can work with a talk therapist is especially helpful. His goal that the person with OCD be able to develop and rely on a network of trusted and reliable human resources is surprisingly similar to Catholic concepts of Communion and Providence.

Obsessive Compulsive Disorder Foundation. 1989–present. *OCD Newsletter.* Milford, Conn.: OCD Foundation. This highly informative newsletter is published approximately six times each year. It is particularly helpful with information concerning medication, behavior therapy, and support groups. Over the years there have been some excellent articles on OCD in combination with such afflictions as attention deficit hyperactivity disorders, eating disorders, Tourette's syndrome, and trichtillomania. There have also been articles concerning scrupulosity and spirituality. Many articles are written by sufferers of OCD themselves and this first-hand perspective is not only informative but provides healing with the message "you are not alone."

Obsessive Compulsive Disorder Foundation. 1993. *The Touching Tree* (videotape). Milford, Conn.: OCD Foundation. This is a very touching story about a boy who is obsessed with touching a certain tree. Grown-ups have left him feeling weird and strange. This forty-minute videotape has won a number of awards. Adults with scrupulosity may be helped to see how and when their scrupulosity began.

O'Flaherty, F. 1965. *How to Cure Scruples.* Milwaukee: Bruce Publishing. This is a highly readable and very practical account of how to deal with and treat scrupulosity. Father O'Flaherty is literate, humorous, and compassionate. While this book may not be available commercially, it can often be obtained through interlibrary loan from the collections of Catholic colleges or seminaries.

Pharm Ethics, Inc. 1996. *OCD — When a Habit Isn't Just a Habit: A Guide to Obsessive-Compulsive Disorder.* Pinebrook, N.J.: CIBA-Geigy Pharmaceuticals. This twenty-eight-page pamphlet was sent to licensed psychiatrists and psychologists when Anafranil (Chlorimipramine) was approved by the FDA for use in the United States for OCD. The booklet provides data concerning the effectiveness of Anafranil, and there is useful information on side effects as well as studies in the psychopharmacological journals.

Roy, C. 1993. *Obsessive Compulsive Disorder: A Survival Guide for Family and Friends.* New Hyde Park, N.Y. A short and helpful guide for families based on the Twelve Steps of AA-type self-help programs. There is an excellent chapter on how the Twelve Steps apply to OCD. This chapter includes some written exercises which could be very helpful for OCD sufferers themselves.

Scrupulous Anonymous, Liguori, MO 63057-9999. This excellent organization links nearly ten thousand persons who suffer from scrupulosity. They come from all fifty states and many foreign countries. A four-page monthly newsletter is sent to members. Themes from this letter often focus on healthy spirituality and developing a clear and prudent moral sense. Some of the most helpful discussions center on "dilemmas" sent in by readers. These are followed by careful and helpful responses.

Schwartz, J. 1996. *Brain Lock: Free Yourself from Obsessive Compulsive Behavior.* New York: HarperCollins. This is a pioneering book documenting the use of brain imaging approaches in understanding OCD. In a down-to-earth style many interesting case studies are presented.

Salzman, L. 1994. *Treating the Obsessive Compulsive Personality.* An eminent psychoanalyst, Dr. Salzman is the former president of the American Psychoanalytic Association and has been affiliated with Georgetown University Medical School and the Rockville Centre Catholic Marriage Tribunal. The first edition of his book was published in 1968. Despite the batterings psychoanalysts have endured concerning their treatment of OCD, Dr. Salzman stands firm in his belief that there are underlying characteristics of OCD which need more attention than behavior therapy and medication can provide. He does, however, acknowledge in the preface to this latest edition that medication and behavior therapy have proven to be very helpful. This book may be of most interest to professional therapists as it provides an extremely detailed and accurate phenomenology of OCD. It provides many helpful approaches for the professional therapist, which could be adapted by others such as pastoral counselors. Dr. Salzman's book has recently been reissued in paperback and, interestingly, was available at the OCD Conference in Boston, 1995.

Van Kaam, A., and S. Muto. 1993. *The Power of Appreciation.* New York: Crossroad. The approach by these noted authors in spirituality could be classified as a cognitive approach to spiritual healing. Many of the ideas concerning personal and relational healing are relevant and helpful to people with scrupulosity. There is an excellent collection of aphorisms in the section "Affirmations for Appreciative Living."

Vertullo, Christine. *OCD-List.* Marist College. <JZID@MARISTB.MARIST.EDU> The OCD-L list was founded to discuss issues concerning obsessive compulsive disorder. Discussions of any topic directly related to how OCD affects life are welcome. People with OCD are invited to join as well as family and friends of OCD persons. Health professionals are also encouraged to subscribe and share their knowledge with the participants. Archives are kept in monthly files. To subscribe, send the following command in the BODY of the mail to LIST-SERV@MARIST.BITNET or LISTSERV@VM.MARIST.EDU on the Internet.

REFERENCES

Abata, R. 1976. *Helps for the Scrupulous*. Liguori, Mo.: Liguori Publications.

Adler, M. J. 1966. *The Difference of Man and the Difference It Makes*. New York: Fordham University Press.

American Psychiatric Association. 1992. *Diagnostic and Statistical Manual of Mental Disorders IV*. Washington, D.C.: American Psychiatric Association Press.

Aquinas, T. *Summa Theologica; Summa Contra Gentiles*.

Ahrens, S., and G. Deffner. 1986. "Empirical Study of Alexithymia: Methodology and Results." *American Journal of Psychiatry* 40, no. 3 (July): 430–47.

Askin, H., Y. Paultre, R. White, and W. Van Ornum. 1993. "Scrupulosity in the General Population." *The 101st Meeting of the American Psychological Association*. Toronto, August 18, 1993.

Baars, C. W., and A. A. Turruwe. 1981. *Psychic Wholeness and Healing: Using All the Powers of the Human Psyche*. Staten Island, N.Y.: Alba House.

Bell, R. M. 1985. *Holy Anorexia*. Chicago: University of Chicago Press.

Benedictine Monks of St. Augustine's Abbey. 1921. *The Book of Saints: A Dictionary of Servants of God Canonised by the Catholic Church and Extracted from the Roman and Other Martyrologies*. London: Black, Ltd.

"Brain Wound Eliminates Man's Mental Illness." 1988. *New York Times*. February 25.

Breggin, P. 1991. *Toxic Psychiatry*. New York: St. Martin's.

———. 1993. *Talking Back to Prozac*. New York: Bantam Books.

Brown, R. E. 1994. *The Death of the Messiah: From Gethsemane to the Grave*. New York: Doubleday.

Carson, R., N. Butcher, and S. Benike. 1995. *Abnormal Psychology and Modern Life*. 10th ed. New York: HarperCollins.

Catechism of the Catholic Church. 1994. New York: Doubleday.

Chesterton, G. K. 1965. *Orthodoxy*. New York: Image Books.

Ciarrocchi, J. W. 1995. *The Doubting Disease*. Mahwah, N.J.: Paulist Press.

CIBA-Geigy. 1992. *OCD — When a Habit Isn't Just a Habit: A Guide to Obsessive-Compulsive Disorder*. Pinebrook, N.J.: CIBA-Geigy Pharmaceuticals.

Cohen, R. J. 1995. *Psychological Assessment*. Mayfield, Calif.: Mayfield Publishing Co.

Emmelkamp, P. M. 1982. *Phobic and Obsessive Compulsive Disorders*. New York: Plenum.

Erikson, E. 1958. *Young Man Luther: A Study in Psychoanalysis and History.* New York: W. W. Norton.

Festinger, Trudy. 1984. *No One Ever Asked Us.* New York: Child Welfare Association of America.

Foa, E., and R. Wilson. 1991. *Stop Obsessing: How to Overcome Your Obsessions and Compulsions.* New York: Bantam Books.

Freud, S. 1963. *Three Case Histories: The Wolf Man, The Rat Man, and the Psychotic Dr. Schreiber.* New York: Macmillan.

Gemelli, A. 1913. *De Scrupulis: Psychopathologiae Specimen in Usum Confessariorum.* Florence, Italy: Libreria Editrice Fiorentina.

Giordano, J. 1995. "Culture Implications for Family Therapists." *APA Monitor,* October: 38–40.

Girzone, J. F. 1987. *Joshua.* New York: Scribners.

Greenburg, D., E. Witztum, and J. Pisante. 1987. "Scrupulosity: Religious Attitudes and Clinical Presentation." *British Journal of Medical Psychology* 60:29–37.

Gritsch, E. W. 1983. *Martin — God's Court Jester: Luther in Retrospect.* Philadelphia: Fortress Press.

Huizinga, J. 1957. *Erasmus and the Age of Reformation.* New York: Scribner's.

James, W. 1982. *The Varieties of Religious Experience: A Study in Human Nature.* New York: Penguin Books.

John Paul II, Pope. 1994. *Crossing the Threshold of Hope.* New York: Macmillan.

Kübler-Ross, E. 1981. *Living with Death and Dying.* New York: Macmillan.

Levenkron, S. 1991. *Obsessive Compulsive Disorder.* New York: Warner Books.

Levinson, H. S. 1981. *The Religious Investigations of William James.* New York: Basic Books.

Livingston, B. 1989. *Learning to Live with Obsessive Compulsive Disorders.* Milford, Conn.: OCD Foundation.

Martyn, W. C. 1866. *The Life and Times of Martin Luther.* New York: American Tract Society.

Mattola, A. 1964. *The Spiritual Exercises of St. Ignatius.* New York: Doubleday Image Books.

McLean, J. M., and S. A. Knights. 1989. *Phobics and Other Panic Victims.* New York: Continuum.

Meissner, W. W. 1992. *Ignatius of Loyola: The Psychology of a Saint.* New Haven: Yale University Press.

Minuchin, S. 1967. *Families of the Slums.* New York: Basic Books.

Mordock, J. B. 1991. *Counseling the Defiant Child.* New York: Crossroad.

Mowrer, H. O. 1952. "Neurosis and Psychotherapy." In O. H. Mowrer, *Psychotherapy Research and Practice.* New York: Ronald Press, 78–99.

Neziroglu, F., and J. A. Yaryura-Tobias. 1994. "Obsessive Compulsive Disorder." In J. Ronch, W. Van Ornum, and N. Stilwell, eds., *The Counseling Source Book: A Practical Reference on Contemporary Issues.* New York: Crossroad, 428–40.

O'Flaherty, V. M. 1966. *How to Cure Scruples.* Milwaukee: Bruce Publishing Company.

Paul VI, Pope. 1972. *Sacram Unctionem Infirmorum*. In A. Flannery, *Vatican Council II: More Post-conciliar Documents*. Collegeville, Minn.: Liturgical Press, 1982, 13–14.

Penzel, F. 1995. "Obsessive Fears of Homosexuality." *OCD Newsletter* (October): 5–6.

Rapoport, J. L. 1990. *The Boy Who Couldn't Stop Washing: The Experience and Treatment of Obsessive Compulsive Disorder*. New York: New American Library.

Rauch, S. L., and M. A. Jenike. 1993. "Neuro-biological Models of Obsessive Compulsive Disorder." *Psychosomatics* 34, no. 1 (January–February 1993): 20–26.

Salzman, L. 1994. *Treatment of Obsessive and Compulsive Behaviors*. London: Jason Aronson.

Scrupulous Anonymous Newsletter. Liguori, Mo.: Liguori Publications.

Steinhorn, A., and A. McDonald. 1990. *Understanding Homosexuality*. New York: Continuum.

Steketee, G., and K. White. 1990. *When Once Is Not Enough: Help for Obsessive Compulsives*. Oakland, Calif.: New Harbinger Publications.

Thompson, M. W., R. R. McInnes, and H. F. Willard. 1991. *Genetics in Medicine*. 5th ed. Philadelphia: Saunders.

Van Ornum, W., and J. B. Mordock. 1991. *Crisis Counseling with Children and Adolescents*. New York: Crossroad.

Van Ornum, W., H. Askin, Y. Paultre, and R. White. 1990. "Obsessive Compulsive Disorder and Scrupulosity: A Preliminary Investigation." *The 98th Annual Meeting of the American Psychological Association*, Boston, August 21, 1990.

———. 1992. "Construct and Concurrent Validity for a Scale of Scrupulosity and Obsessive Compulsive Disorder." *The 100th Annual Meeting of the American Psychological Association*, Washington, D.C., August 14, 1992.

Weil, S. 1951. *Waiting for God*. New York: G. P. Putnam's Sons.

Williamson, M. 1994. *Illuminata: A Return to Prayer*. New York: Riverhead Press.

Wright, A. G. 1990. "Ecclesiastes (Qoheleth)." In R. Brown, J. Fitzmyer, and R. Murphy, *The New Jerome Biblical Commentary*. Englewood Cliffs, N.J.: Prentice-Hall, 489–95.

Zraly, K., and D. Swift. 1991. *Anorexia, Bulimia, and Compulsive Overeating*. New York: Continuum.

INDEX

OF RELATED INTEREST

John Jacob Raub

WHO TOLD YOU THAT YOU WERE NAKED?
Freedom from Judgment, Guilt, and Fear of Punishment

Readers are sure to find peace in this consoling call to overcome feelings of guilt that come from our illusion that we are separate from the love of God. The author shows us how it is only our belief in the God who loves us as we are — not as we should be — that brings us freedom from guilt and fear.

"The book has a strong message, at once consoling and convincing, which all of us will be the better — and the happier — for hearing."
— Msgr. William Shannon,
author of *Seeking the Face of God*

"A healing balm. It deserves a wide readership."
— Brother Patrick Hart, O.C.S.O.

0-8245-1203-0; $11.95

At your bookstore or, to order directly from the publisher, please send check or money order (including $3.00 shipping for the first book and $1.00 for each additional book) to:

THE CROSSROAD PUBLISHING COMPANY
370 LEXINGTON AVENUE, NEW YORK, NY 10017

We hope you enjoyed A Thousand Frightening Fantasies.
Thank you for reading it.

crossroad